StyleCity
NEW YORK

StyleCity

NEW YORK

NEW EDITION

With over 350 colour photographs and 7 maps

Contents

Street Wise

Style Traveler

Series concept and editor: Lucas Dietrich
Research and author: Alice Twemlow
Original design concept: The Senate
Jacket and book design: Grade Design Consultants
Maps: Peter Bull

Specially commissioned photography by
Ingrid Rasmussen, Anthony Webb and Yoko Inoue

The StyleCity series is a completely independent guide.

Every effort has been made to ensure that the
information in this book is as up-to-date and as
accurate as possible at the time of going to press,
but some details are liable to change.

First published in the United Kingdom in 2003 by
Thames & Hudson Ltd, 181A High Holborn,
London WC1V 7QX

www.thamesandhudson.com

British Library Cataloguing-in-Publication Data
A catalogue record for this book is available from the
British Library

ISBN 13: 978-0-500-21018-5
ISBN 10: 0-500-21018-7

Printed in China by C & C Offset Printing Co Ltd

How to Use This Guide

The book features two principal sections: **Street Wise** and **Style Traveler**.

Street Wise, which is arranged by neighborhood, features areas that can be covered in a day (and night) on foot and includes a variety of locations – cafés, shops, restaurants, museums, performance spaces, bars – that capture local flavor or are lesser-known destinations.

The establishments in the **Style Traveler** section represent the city's best and most characteristic locations – "worth a detour" – and feature hotels (**sleep**), restaurants (**eat**), cafés and bars (**drink**), boutiques and shops (**shop**) and getaways (**retreat**).

Each location is shown as a circled number on the relevant neighborhood map, which is intended to provide a rough idea of location and proximity to major sights and landmarks rather than precise position. Locations in each neighborhood are presented sequentially by map number. Each entry in the **Style Traveler** has two numbers: the top one refers to the page number of the neighborhood map on which it appears; the second number is its location.

For example, the visitor might begin by selecting a hotel from the **Style Traveler** section. Upon arrival, **Street Wise** might lead him to the best joint for coffee before guiding him to a house-museum nearby. After lunch he might go to find a special jewelry store listed in the **shop** section. For a memorable dining experience, he might consult his neighborhood section to find the nearest restaurant crossreferenced to **eat** in **Style Traveler**.

Street addresses are given in each entry, and complete information – including email and web addresses – is listed in the alphabetical **contact** section. Travel and contact details for the destinations in **retreat** are given at the end of **contact**.

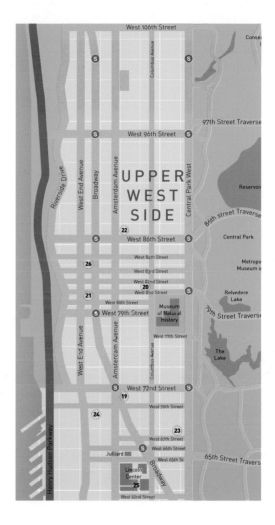

Legend

(2)	Location
▪	Museums, sights
▪	Gardens, squares
Ⓢ	Subway
▪	Streets

NEW YORK

To Walt Whitman in "City of Ships," New York was a "Proud and passionate city! Mettlesome, mad, extravagant city!" The refrain of E. B. White's poignant 1949 essay "Here is New York" is "the essential fever of New York." Architect Rem Koolhaas's 1978 socio-architectural analysis of New York is titled *Delirious New York*, and it's not just a conceit. The recurring reference to mania in the various literary, musical and artistic responses to the city throughout its history is hardly surprising: New York is as much a sensibility as it is a topographically defined area. Temperatures, temperaments, expectations and spectacles are exaggerated in this densely packed can of about eight million sardines. The biggest bagels, the fastest taxi cabs, the biggest economic disparity, the skinniest lattes — it's truly a city of superlatives.

Unlike most other contemporary metropolises, Manhattan cannot sprawl and become a conurbation. Two rivers confine its expansion to the vertical axis. It can move upwards and it can transplant attitudinal seedlings to the outer boroughs, but growth mainly occurs in a folding fashion, in and on top of itself. The friction generated by this "culture of congestion," as Koolhaas dubbed it, is both New York's virtue and its vice. Creation and destruction go hand in hand in a city that is in a constant state of renewal. Just as in 1947, when the architect Le Corbusier wrote, "New York is not a completed city, it is a city in the process of becoming," today's city continues to demolish and build itself, expanding into and reinventing new neighborhoods, discarding others at dizzying velocity. The most visible of the construction sites is an area of Lower Manhattan, popularly known as Ground Zero, which is currently being shaped to Polish-born and Bronx-bred architect Daniel Libeskind's 1,776-foot-tall (840-meter) vision.

Catalyzing this creative cauldron are the combined visions of restaurateurs, club promoters, designers, boutique curators and gallerists who are constantly pushing at the boundaries of neighborhoods and their lifestyle culture. In a given neighborhood's renewal it is the period of transition when feverish renovation grinds against day-to-day life of the area's inhabitants that is the most fascinating and highly charged. The "completeness" of a locale's transformation is always its death knell. Luc Sante has characterized New York as a city where "the navel of the world and the frontier of civilization lie a few blocks apart. And therein lies its energy."

While the surface of the city is continually undergoing cosmetic surgery – a global-brand store tuck here and an injection of Botox to banish the drug addicts there – the substructure of old and fantastical Gotham is never far away. Steam wheezes out of manholes, a reminder of the city's ancient heating system. You can glimpse traces of painted advertising signage on the walls of buildings. In the summer children play in the jets of water hydrants as if in a 1930s Weegee photograph, and subway air-vents near the Flatiron building still send skirts flying.

New York, and specifically Manhattan, is a walking city. At 13.5 by 2.5 miles wide (21.5 by 4 kilometers) at 14th Street, it is possible to traverse much of Manhattan's length and breadth in a day. There are many ways of walking ranging from the corporate executive's streamlined march to the self-evolved wide-legged shuffle of Lower East Side kids, whose movements are restricted by the need to prevent their low-slung pants from falling off. On the whole, the walking is of a speed unmatched by other cities. This pace, just like the reasoning behind the "212" dialling code for Manhattan – the numerals are the closest together on the telephone dial pad, making it the speediest code to dial – are necessitated by the brevity of the New York minute.

At the risk of annoying native street-walkers, as a first-time or repeat visitor to the city you might try a particularly fine mode of transport originally expounded by Situationist Guy Debord in 1958: "drifting," or "a technique of rapid passage through varied ambiences" is still a superior way in which to absorb a city's "psychogeographical contours." As you walk, allow yourself to be free of life's ordinary motivations. Be drawn by your instinct, send your gaze upward, allow yourself to overhear conversations – whether its the loud-mouthed, wisecracking exchange between deli-server and customer or an aesthetic difference in opinion between a lady-who-lunches and her personal shopper in Bergdorf Goodman.

This book offers ideas for staging posts along the paths of your forays. In the following pages you will find exceptional designed environments and experiences that are idiosyncratic to New York and stylish in unconventional ways. They range from classic 19th-century spit-and-sawdust saloons, Jewish delicatessens and gas-lit chophouses that have withstood the churn of constant urban renewal, to the sleek lounges, chic cafés, exquisitely assembled boutiques and utterly contemporary hotels that are heralded as bastions of cool. If there is a unifying gesture in the eclectic spectrum of New York's most exuberant play-spaces and refined oases for repose, then it is panache. Extreme panache.

Street Wise

TriBeCa • Chinatown • Little Italy • NoLIta • SoHo • NoHo • Chelsea • Meatpacking District • West Village • Gramercy Park • East Village • Lower East Side • Lower Manhattan • Midtown • Upper East Side • Upper West Side • Harlem • Williamsburg • Long Island City • DUMBO • Park Slope • Smith Street • Fort Greene

TriBeCa

Chinatown

Little Italy

NoLIta

SoHo

NoHo

New York is a city of transitioning neighborhoods and nowhere is their ebb and flow more apparent than in the acronym-happy villages below and around Houston Street. The once-decaying industrial area now known as TriBeCa (Triangle Below Canal) began to be converted into residential lofts in the late 1970s by artists deserting SoHo because of rising rents. Over the following two decades, A-listers – Robert De Niro among them – snapped up gargantuan lofts in late 19th-century cast-iron buildings and the area's population increased exponentially. Chic eateries soon followed, and today the area is completely gentrified, with a host of furniture and architectural salvage stores and a sprinkling of fashion boutiques.

The sudden shift from one community to the next within the space of a block is continually startling. One minute you are walking in a sea of red plastic bags, the unofficial logos of Chinatown's food markets, and the next you are hit by the smell of salami and coffee wafting out of one of the remaining Italian fine-food stores. There are few places in Little Italy that still give a sense of its storied past: the Ravenite Social Club on Mulberry Street, for example, which was celebrity don John Gotti's headquarters from the mid-1980s until his arrest in 1990, is now a handbag and accessories store. But there are some that still give you a whiff, albeit a friendlier one, of what it used to be like on these mean streets. The district known as NoLIta (North of Little Italy) is the area with the highest concentration of new boutiques and Europhile cafés. These businesses sprang up in the late 1990s and, in a heartbeat, displaced a Sicilian community. The term NoLIta describes a fashionable lifestyle as much as it does a geographical area.

SoHo was the center of New York's art scene from the 1970s until the mid-1990s when chain stores started to move in, raising the rents, ousting old stalwarts and pushing the more interesting stores and galleries to areas outside its perimeter. Although SoHo's heyday has long since passed, the beauty of the area's distinctive cast-iron buildings with their zigzag fire escapes, the bottle-glass sidewalks that allow light into storage vaults below, streets of Belgian brick and traces of Jean-Michel Basquiat's graffiti heritage here and there can cause you to forget for a second the rude invasion of global brands.

Hiding to the east of the strip-mall of lower Broadway and continuing north of Houston Street is a little-spoilt oasis called NoHo, with Bond Street as its primary spokes-street. The ground floors of 19th-century loft buildings with façades of marble, cast iron, limestone and terracotta are largely returned to their original usage as retail stores.

TIMELESS ELEGANCE

2 **Chanterelle**

2 Harrison Street

This grandly proportioned space, once the site of the Mercantile Exchange, was remodeled in 1989 by owners Bill Katz and Karen Waltuck into an elegant, airy dining room. Seemingly immune to the vagaries of fashion influencing its TriBeCa neighbors, Chanterelle has retained the same classic interior ever since. Its features include magnificent floral arrangements, and widely spaced tables set simply with white linen and china. Large windows are half covered with sheer curtains, and the reception area walls are hung with artworks by the likes of Cindy Sherman and Cy Twombly. The menu, which changes every four weeks, features hearty French dishes such as beef fillet with oysters and oyster sauce.

VAULTED GASTRONOMY

3 **Bouley**

120 West Broadway

Twelve-foot (4-meter) half-moon windows, low Guastavino-style vaulted ceilings hung with chandeliers and walls painted blood red provide a suitably dramatic setting for chef David Bouley's culinary spectacles. The five-course tasting menu includes an appetizer called "Return from Chiang Mai" that features chilled Maine lobster, mango, fresh artichoke, Serrano ham and passion fruit, fresh coconut and Kaffir lime dressing.

URBAN IDYLL

4 **Duane Park**

Duane Street and Hudson Street

Nestled in the middle of a busy intersection in TriBeCa is an unexpected green triangle of calm and beauty. New York's second oldest public park has the active support of locals, who look after its historical importance and keep it fresh with new plantings. Lying at the heart of TriBeCa, it also provides a good vantage point from which to observe the richly detailed brick buildings that surround it.

BRIGHT LIGHTS, BIG CITY

5 **Odeon**

SCULPTING FASHION

7 TriBeCa Issey Miyake
119 Hudson Street

This store, on the ground floor of a TriBeCa cast-iron building, carries Miyake's womens- and menswear lines, including his experimental A-POC clothing, and all of the accompanying accessories and fragrances. Frank Gehry collaborated with the architecture firm G Tects to create the titanium wave that dominates the store's interior. Many of the techniques used for the Bilbao Guggenheim were applied here to create the billows and curves of the metallic structure that offsets the Japanese designer's convention-busting wares.

ART ENTERPRISE

8 Gavin Brown's Enterprise
620 Greenwich Street

Elusive Brit art dealer Gavin Brown chooses to position Enterprise just outside the fashionable concentration of galleries. As soon as other spaces invaded his original south-of-Chelsea territory, he upped sticks and moved even further down Manhattan to an out-of-the way location at the bottom end of the West Village. But with a continually fresh roster of Young British Artists and American up-and-comers including Urs Fischer, Martin Creed, Laura Owens, Elizabeth Peyton and Rob Pruitt, collectors and critics are never far behind.

SPEAKEASY VIBES

9 Employees Only
156

NOT JUST ANOTHER BAR

10 Another Room
249 West Broadway

A good selection of interesting and reasonably priced beers and international wines can be found at this enduring and unaffected TriBeCa bar. Dark and candlelit in winter, breezy and spilling out onto the sidewalk in summer, Another Room's laid-back, homey ambiance is perpetuated by the combination of owner Craig Weiss's vision, an unpretentious staff with good taste in independent music, and a local crowd happy to escape the tyranny of the velvet rope.

DEPARTMENT STORE, CHINESE STYLE

11 Pearl River Mart

477 Broadway

Household wares that span the spectrum from exotic chic to practical necessity are crazily crammed into the two floors of this Chinese department store. Join a melee of Chinese grannies buying electric rice cookers and hip young women finding accessories for their NoLIta boutiques. Jostle for t'ai chi slippers, beaded flip-flops and dragon-embroidered jackets, paper goods and brilliantly decorated porcelain tea mugs.

STREET ARCHITECTURE

12 Storefront for Art and Architecture

97 Kenmare Street

Designed by Steven Holl and Vito Acconci in 1993, this gallery space for architectural thought and practice bursts beyond its tiny slice-of-pie footprint. The irregularly rectilinear plates in the concrete-board façade revolve on vertical and horizontal pivots so they can flip open to the street, making the space an exercise in mutable architecture.

PEOPLE-WATCHING AND COFFEE

13 Caffé Roma

| 154 |

UNDERGROUND SCENE

14 Double Happiness

173 Mott Street

In former incarnations, Double Happiness was a speak-easy, a shady Italian restaurant and a mob-run gay bar. Today, the basement bar, along with the newly opened Happy Ending on nearby Broome Street, is the scenic backdrop for a bevy of beautiful people bopping to the strains of regular DJs as they sip on their green-tea Martini house specials. The interior incorporates a giant abacus as a window between two sections of the bar and there is a variety of seating options beneath the open brickwork arches.

DESTINATION CHINESE CLASSICS

15 Peking Duck House

28 Mott Street

The interior is unusually minimal for a Chinese restaurant. But once you are served your platters of delicately crisp duck skin with stacks of house-made pancakes, and green scallions, fresh cucumbers and special hoisin sauce, you won't be looking up again to notice. The bring-your-own wine policy and reasonably priced food mean that a large group can eat handsomely for less than $15 a head.

THE BOHEMIAN VIBE

16 Knitting Factory

74 Leonard Street

New York's downtown experimental music establishment is a honeycomb of rooms and bars on four floors that on any one night might be hosting an alternative film festival, jazz in the Tap Room, hip-hop poetry readings or performances by the likes of John Lury, Sonic Youth or Carl Craig. The main performance space, with an intimate capacity of only 250, is a great place to see up-and-coming bands in a seriously bohemian setting.

HOTEL BAR REDEFINED

17 Church Lounge

TriBeCa Grand Hotel, 2 Sixth Avenue

Instead of a restaurant, the TriBeCa Grand offers casual dining in the various plush seating areas scattered throughout its large atrium. In the evening, the left side of the triangular bar, especially the semi-private Chambers Lounge, becomes a hot spot. The DJ program is consistently good – spin guests include the Eighteenth Street Lounge heavyweights Thunderball and Blue States – and some of the most glamorous parties are held here – Fischerspooner's after-show party recently filled the lounge with leg-warmer-wearing Electroclash groupies.

CAFÉ CULTURE

18 Café Gitane

| 146 |

VELVET UNDERGROUND

19 I Heart

| 175 |

FEMININE WILES

20 Mayle

| 173 |

HANDMADE SHIRTS

21 Seize sur Vingt

| 171 |

Bounded by the Bowery to the east, Lafayette to the west, Houston to the north and overlapping with Little Italy to the south is the province known as NoLIta. Mott, Mulberry and Elizabeth Streets, in particular, are lined with meticulously curated boutiques that open and close like so many pretty butterflies. Albanese Meats and Poultry, sitting resiliently in a street now recast by trend-setting young retailers, is an original relic from a time when the area was a Sicilian enclave.

If you can get (and keep) a table at this buzzing corner luncheonette, use it as your NoLIta model-watching HQ. The nuevo-Mexican/Cuban menu offers a range of spicy dishes, but the grilled corncob rolled in grated cotija cheese and chilli powder and sprinkled with lime juice is the one the regulars go for.

Hand-painted, banana-leaf wallpaper lines the walls (you can buy rolls of it at the desk), the music is just right, and there is a stylish range of casual T-shirts, anoraks and trousers in this tasty morsel of a menswear boutique.

With its blossom-patterned wallpaper, red booths and paucity of tables (there are only nine), this gorgeous NoLIta café resembles a 1930s Little Italy lunch counter. The kitchen serves low-priced pan-Asian comfort food, such as chicken satay, Pad Thai and steamed dumplings.

With her collection of floral dresses and sparkly, strappy shoes and accessories, designer, storeowner and hostess Holly Dunlap attempts to recreate the sunshiny vibe of 1970s California pool parties. The nostalgia continues throughout the store's cabanna-like interior, festively decked out with crystal chandeliers and wicker stools.

This small dress shop run by designer Emma Fletcher carries her own line of feminine dresses, velvet jackets and flouncy silk-chiffon blouses, alongside her picks of vintage clothes, shoes and jewelry. Fletcher uses a stamped-tin ceiling and authentic 1940s wallpaper to create an evocative yet understated setting, in contrast to many of her glitzy, glammed-up neighbors.

INA is the civilized choice for designer consignment shopping. In an atmosphere that is far more refined than the meltdown-inducing Century 21, you'll find an array of discerningly picked designer clothes, accessories and shoes in pristine condition – some are samples. INA's self-described purpose is to "select only what's in fashion from those who are in fashion for those who want to be in fashion." Join other NoLIta girls and boys who spent too much on their brunch for a rummage through the racks that burst with wares from the likes of Helmut Lang, Prada, Vivienne Westwood and Kors.

COUTURE MAGAZINE'S GALLERY
36 Visionaire
11 Mercer Street

This small gallery puts on curated shows and reflects the inspiration and process behind the irregularly appearing and limited-edition *Visionaire* album. Conceived by Stephan Gan, Cecilia Dean and James Kaliardos, this couture version of a regular magazine has taken various forms and involved luminaries from the worlds of fashion, art and design. A recent issue, titled *Love*, was created from 4,000 hardcover novels, hand-assembled with inserts from Björk, Matthew Barney, Nick Knight, Mario Testino, Philip Treacy and Jonathan Safran Foer, to name a few – and finished with a sterling-silver heart on a black silk cord by legendary jewelry designer Elsa Peretti for Tiffany & Co.

THE SOHO BRASSERIE EPITOMIZED
37 Balthazar
80 Spring Street

Even if you don't have time for a multistory iced-shellfish platter at this infamous SoHo brasserie, make sure you do, at the very least, breeze in and out, either to pick up a croissant in the adjoining pint-sized patisserie or for a bowl of steaming café au lait in the bar area. Worn red leather banquettes, age-spotted mirrors and nicotine-stained paint were used to create an already aged French bistro look in this airy 180-table space. "I didn't have in mind a particular restaurant in France that I was trying to imitate," says owner Keith McNally, "but there are bits and experiences of various restaurants that have stuck with me." Balthazar is one of those contemporary SoHo landmarks – others include the Prada store, Dean and Deluca, the window of Pleats Please, the bathroom at Bar 89 – that you just have to see; they are part of the deal.

SUBLIME HANDCRAFTED JEWELRY
38 Ted Muehling
27 Howard Street

Pay homage to craftsmanship and beauty at this minimal store dissembling as a gallery space. Muehling's sculptural jewelry is inspired by organic forms such as shells, rocks, coral, eggs and berries. The pared-down shapes are exquisitely rendered in brushed gold or finely hammered metal. His delicate ceramic work is manufactured at the Nymphenburg porcelain factory in Germany, and all of the pieces are displayed simply in tall glass cases.

BATHROOM LIGHTS FANTASTIC
39 Bar 89
89 Mercer Street

While the cocktails are large and powerful and the menu of bar snacks appealing, it is Bar 89's bathroom on the balcony that gives cause for real delight. The doors to the unisex stalls are seemingly transparent until you close the latch and the glass becomes opaque.

CURATORIAL EXPERIMENTATION
40 Artists Space
38 Greene Street, 3rd Floor

A pioneer in the alternative-space movement, Artists Space was founded in 1972 as a non-profit institution supporting contemporary artists. Today the gallery is one of the few exhibition spaces to exploit the dynamic interchange between practice that involves design, video, performance, architecture and art. In its 25-year history, Artists Space has presented the work of over 5,000 emerging artists.

APE FOR TENNIES
41 A Bathing Ape
91 Greene Street

An unmarked location, no website, and carefully controlled quantities of stock are some of the more unusual techniques Japanese designer and sometime DJ Nigo uses to promote Bathing Ape. His candy-hued sneakers, influenced by old-school hip hop and worn by contemporary rappers Jay-Z, Cassidy and Pharrell, among others, are the main attractions of his new minimalist store as they rotate on a conveyor belt in the window. Inside, you'll find a pared-down assortment of urban streetwear, accessories and limited-edition toys.

This five-story building on the northeast corner of Spring and Mercer Streets was purchased in 1968 by the Archdeacon of Minimalism, furniture maker and artist, Donald Judd. The 1870 cast-iron building is now managed by Judd's estate. You can look through the ground-floor windows and see some of Judd's pieces, as well as the work of Carl Andre and Dan Flavin, two of the artists whose work he collected. While the inaccessibility of the building's interior may be frustrating, it's a lot easier than traveling to Marfa, Texas, the town that Judd has transformed into an art installation.

Follow the skateboarders to this fresh little store that stocks t-shirts, sweats and shoes from Goodenough, DC shoes, Analog, Burton, Gravis, Girl, Chocolate, as well as the store's own label. The video wall, Futura artwork and display of decks – including Supreme's own PMS paint-chip design – is its own art gallery. For more skate togs on the same street, try Triple Five Soul (no. 290) or X-Large (no. 265).

Catering to all your urban vinyl, 12-inch action figure, and plush toy needs, this emporium for grown-up kids contains glass case-loads of cute and badass characters like Smorkin' Hate Dunny (an 8-inch Pepto-Bismol pink rabbit with a 5 o'clock shadow and cigarette) and Babo the Uglydoll by artists David Horvath and Sun-Min Kim. When yet another Statue of Liberty snow globe just won't do, take home a toy by a New York City graffiti artist such as Quik, Dalek, Tristan, Lase NYC, Filth or Dr. Revolt.

Some of the most ambitious presentations of emerging art, design and music take place in Jeffrey Deitch's two SoHo project spaces. With an A-list of international artists and friends at Deitch's beck and call – Vanessa Beecroft, Fischerspooner, Chris Johanson, Barry McGee, Mariko Mori and 1980s legend Keith Haring among them – the experimental gallery owner is able to assemble shows that enchant even the most jaded of New York's "artgentsia." The Wooster space, the size of a garage, hosts occasional site-specific installations and performances – a recent show, "Session the Bowl," featured a kidney-shaped skating bowl, replete with skaters, by the artist collective Simparch. The more intimate Grand Street gallery is home to a regular program of exhibits.

If you feel that your hotel room distances you from the way your contemporaries live in this city, then take a trip to The Apartment, a store designed to make you feel right at home – albeit a rather idealized home. The owners, Gina Alverez and Stefan Boublil, have divided the two-floor space into areas that represent a living room, office, bedroom, kitchen, bathroom and closet. Didier Chaudanson's snap-together lights, Freecell's tractor chairs and Kenyan Lewis's fly riding caps can all be found in the appropriate room, and sometimes you can pick up coffee and snacks in the kitchen.

Fanelli's has been serving food and drink in inimitable, no-nonsense style since 1847. This genuine bar, incongruous in its central SoHo location, has managed to weather a fashion tempest that has swept along Prince Street, leaving bland chain stores in its desultory wake. Bob the bartender is a retired prizefighter and a wall of original boxing photographs and portraits from the early 1900s pay tribute to the pugilist's art.

With a colorful Vacation in your hand (the bar's signature drink, available in pink, green or blue), you are ready to lounge on a brocaded ottoman or the long cowhide couch in this classic SoHo watering hole. The fabulousness of the rustic but comfortable mountain lodge-style bar is nicely faded like a pair of well-worn jeans. John McDonald, the restaurateur, owns both the Merc Bar and the Marc Newson–designed Lever House Restaurant (p. 143) in Midtown. He is also the editor and publisher of the design, fashion and food rag, *City NY*, a stylish magazine McDonald sees as the American take on *Wallpaper**.

50 Vesuvio Bakery Shop
160 Prince Street

Established in 1920 by Neopolitan immigrants, the bakery was run by their son, "unofficial mayor of Greenwich Village" Anthony Dapolito, until it was sold in 2003 to a pair of local sisters-in-law. Its gold-stencilled window still displays homemade Italian bread and *tarellas* (pepper biscuits) in spite of the enforced evacuation of nearly all of SoHo's other mom-and-pop shops.

HALF-MILE OF BRASS RODS
51 Broken Kilometer
393 West Broadway

Viewing land artist Walter de Maria's installation of 500 highly polished, solid brass rods precisely placed in five parallel rows is a strangely ethereal experience.

FRAGRANCE LABORATORY
52 Helmut Lang Perfumerie
81 Greene Street

Gluckman Mayner Architects' store for Helmut Lang provides a suitably hard-edged laboratory setting for the minimal designer's fragrance line. The narrow entry is emphasized by an LED installation by Jenny Holzer that runs the length of the interior along the top of an enameled steel wall.

FASHION SUPERMARKET
53 Kirna Zabete

NATURAL SANCTUARY
54 The New York Earth Room
141 Wooster Street

Created in 1977 by American artist Walter de Maria, this pastoral sculpture consists of one SoHo loft and 250 cubic yards (190 cubic meters) of dark topsoil, weighing 280,000 pounds (127,000 kg).

STATE OF ART
55 The Apple Store
103 Prince Street

Need to check your e-mail? Avoid the charges at passé cybercafés and pop into the Apple Store, where you can log on at one of Apple's latest computers. Aside from the array of state-of-the-art digital cameras, iPods and Mac accessories in this gleaming white space designed by Bohlin Cywinski Jackson and Ronette Riley, there is a "Genius Bar" at which to get your technical questions answered and an amphitheatre where workshops and demonstrations are held.

DESIGN MUSEUM
56 Moss

JAPANESE SOBA RESTAURANT
57 Honmura An
170 Mercer Street

This Japanese restaurant is renowned for the quality of its soba noodles. They are made on the premises from locally bought buckwheat and presented in handsome lacquer boxes, accompanied by various dipping sauces. In a famous *New York Times* review, restaurant critic Ruth Reichl gave the restaurant three stars, a rating previously unheard-of for an "ethnic eatery." The serene walk-up SoHo loft space, which features such Zen touches as floating pools of flowers and ceiling-high displays of twisted branches, was designed by the architectural firm Yui and Bloch Design.

BATHING BEAUTY
58 Red Flower
13 Prince Street

Owner Yael Alkalay, former creative director of Shiseido, is behind this shop devoted to bathtime pleasures. Yuzu mimosa sea algae wash, ginger-grass bamboo scrub, and wild cherry blossom rice buff are just three of the seven signature Red Flower products created to reflect the ritual of Japanese bathing.

MAGAZINES AND MULTI-MEDIA
59 Zakka
147 Grand Street

This store-and-gallery destination features an immaculate selection of graphic art books, as well as clothing, music and stationery. The owner takes particular delight in products of the Japanese subculture and art scene, but Zakka also carries an international mix of titles and brands. Among the most sought-after publications are *Gas Book*, *Stash* and *Idea* magazines. Popular toys are the Kaws series of Companions and Mumbleboy's stuffed dolls.

CAMOUFLAGED STORE

60 Nom de Guerre

640 Broadway

Hidden beneath a Swatch store on Broadway is a collection of rare, discontinued and imported clothing and sneakers, assembled by Isa Saalabi and Holly Harnsongkram of Williamsburg's ISA (p. 163). The army theme continues throughout the bunker-like interior in the form of khaki-draped changing rooms and gunmetal shelving. Labels include such local talents as Yoko Devereaux, Tess Giberson, Asfour and Spawning.

LOUIS SULLIVAN IN NEW YORK

61 Bayard Building

65 Bleecker Street

The only building in New York designed by American master architect Louis Sullivan, the 15-story bright-white edifice is best viewed from the corner of Houston and Crosby Streets. The way in which the terracotta curtain walls are used to express the building's structural steel frame is a classic example of the style Sullivan greatly influenced, the Chicago School.

VERDANT OASIS

62 Liz Christy Garden

Houston Street and Bowery

Thanks to the work of activist Liz Christy, the Green Guerillas and a 30-strong team of volunteers, NoHo's visitors and residents have a surprisingly ample oasis of oxygen emanating from the northeastern bank of Houston Street. The Liz Christy Garden, founded in 1973 as the first community garden in New York, has a pond with fish and red-eared slider turtles, a beehive and a wildflower habitat, a grape arbor, a grove of weeping birch trees and hundreds of varieties of flowering perennials.

EIGHTIES GLAM SCENE

63 B-Bar

DOMESTIC HISTORY PRESERVED

64 Merchant's House Museum

29 East 4th Street

This 1832 row house is among the finest surviving examples of the late Federal and Greek Revival architecture of the period. The city's only preserved 19th-century home – the residence of prosperous merchant Seabury Tredwell and his large family – is situated in what was then a fashionable "uptown" district of the city. Three floors of this fascinating home are available for viewing. And, if asked, the knowledgeable docents will explain the details of the formal parlors that feature identical black-and-gold marble mantelpieces, a stunning Ionic double-column screen and mahogany pocket doors separating the rooms. And don't forget the back garden, an otherworldly retreat, restored to 19th-century specifications.

ACCESSORY PALACE

65 Bond 07

WILD-AT-HEART PERFORMANCES

66 Joe's Pub

425 Lafayette Street

Joe's Pub is the wilder sibling of the Joseph Papp Public Theater (look out for Pentagram partner Paula Scher's bold typographic banners on the exterior of the latter). This contemporary take on the cabaret lounge serves up such avant-garde music as a rock opera featuring singers from They Might Be Giants and Hedwig, and theatrical performances including a Shakespearean evening with Steven Berkoff. The nightly after-hours DJ parties are for a crowd of hipsters of ambiguous sexuality, resplendent with inconceivable haircuts.

DJS' DELIGHT

67 Other Music

15 East 4th Street

Other Music is Manhattan's hands-down best record store, with its stock of unclassifiable musical genres unconventionally (and amusingly) categorized as In, Out, Electronica, La Decadanse, Krautrock, Groove, Psychedelia and Then. Tickets to most of the city's hottest gigs can be purchased here, and look out for in-store performances from the likes of DJ Shadow, Yo La Tengo, Jim O'Rourke, Tindersticks and Mouse On Mars.

CHURCH OF VODKA

68 Temple Bar

Chelsea
Meatpacking District
West Village

Chelsea takes its name from the estate of Captain Thomas Clarke who, in 1750, retired to the then-rural area after winning glory in the French and Indian Wars. He named the estate for the hospital for retired soldiers in London. By the 1850s Clarke's grandson had developed the area into a proto-suburb of elegant brownstones on tree-lined streets. When landfill was used to extend the waterfront by three avenues, the newly claimed land was taken over by piers, garages and warehouses and tenements to house immigrant workers. And thus a division between eastern residential Chelsea and western industrial Chelsea arose. Apart from the addition of huge apartment buildings such as the 1,670-unit London Terrace in 1930 and public housing projects in the 1960s, there are many blocks in the eastern swath of Chelsea that are little changed since Victorian times. The industrial section, however, has undergone an enormous revitalization since a caravan of blue-chip art galleries began to arrive from SoHo in the mid-1990s. Today's Chelsea has the highest concentration of contemporary art galleries in the world in the "white cube" area enclosed by Tenth and Eleventh Avenues and 20th and 26th Streets, as well as fine examples of converted-use buildings such as the Chelsea Market in an old Nabisco factory. Chelsea's vibrant gay community is reflected in the character of many of the restaurants, clubs and stores that stay open late into the night.

To the south and west of Chelsea is the Meatpacking District, a wholesale meat market since the 1930s. Until the late 1990s, when the designer boutiques, start-ups and restaurants began to invade its lockers, its cobbled streets were the daytime hangout for brawny meat packers and the nighttime catwalks of transsexual prostitutes. Today there are fewer than 30 meat dealers operating in the area and one gets the feeling that they will disappear altogether in the next few years.

Continue your wanderings south through the off-grid streets of the West Village, which, with its low Federal and Greek-revival row houses, plentiful parks and specialist stores, truly feels like a village. Greenwich Village, once the stomping ground of rebellious artists, bohemians and intellectuals, and later the seedbed of numerous contemporary social movements such as feminism and gay liberation, is now a commercialized tourist trap. Stick to its western reaches – the narrow streets that criss-cross Hudson Street and Bleecker – for your explorations.

Development of the riverside beyond the West Side Highway has led to the conversion of the decaying piers – which until recently were used by late-night cruisers – into verdant leisure parks, and a pathway now runs the western length of southern Manhattan, to the delight of cyclists, roller-bladers and joggers.

STREET EFFLORESCENCE

1 Flower District

West 28th Street, between Sixth and Seventh Avenues

You can catch the scent of this stretch of 28th Street between Sixth and Seventh Avenues well before you reach it. Ever since the 1870s – when flowers became popular for display in upper-class residences – this area has been home to New York's plant and floral wholesalers. Today it is the smallest and most threatened of the City's few remaining single-trade districts. The vendors, specializing in orchids, silk flowers, topiary trees or florists' supplies, use the sidewalks as an extension of their display space so that they become a patchwork of huge crates of variegated tulips and planters of wheatgrass. Even if you don't have time to enter the tiny stores and jostle with party planners and floral designers, merely walking down the street between the hours of 4:30 a.m. and noon is an olfactory and visual experience that should not be missed.

MONUMENTAL WORKS

2 Gagosian Gallery

555 West 24th Street

Heavyweight dealer Larry Gagosian consummated the art world's newfound love for Chelsea when, in 2000, he moved his gallery from SoHo to West 24th Street. With 20,000 square feet (1,860 square meters) of industrial space to play in, Gagosian's is the largest commercial art gallery in Chelsea. One of the first shows to exploit the monumental proportions of the Gluckman Mayner-designed space was Richard Serra's *Torqued Ellipses*. Such 1980s stars as David Salle and Larry Poons show here, as well as several young British artists, including Damien Hirst, Jenny Saville and the Chapman brothers.

OLD-STYLE ELEGANCE

3 The Biltmore Room

290 Eighth Avenue

Many of the decorative elements in this distinctive old Chelsea supper club were salvaged from the former Biltmore Hotel, near Grand Central Station. Brass-lined French doors, Italian Carrera marble, glass chandeliers, and other Beaux-Arts pieces create an elegant ambience in which to savor executive chef Gary Robins's modern American cuisine.

4 Annex Antiques Fair and Flea Market
Sixth Avenue, between 24th and 26th Streets

For an intriguing archaeological dig into Americana's substrata – with furniture, vintage clothing, vintage jewelry, paintings and quirky antiques particularly well represented – look no further than this collection of weekend flea and antiques markets, centered around 26th Street and Sixth Avenue. Come at sunrise for the choice goods and at dusk for the bargains. Hot-dog vendors hover in the vicinity, but a more pleasant refreshment break can be found at the Antique Café at 65 West 26th Street.

MODERNE CREATIVE CENTER
5 Starrett Lehigh Building
601 West 26th Street

This colossal industrial building was built in 1931 by Russell G. & Walter M. Cory and Yasuo Matsui. It might almost be a streamlined ocean liner grounded on the bank of the Hudson River. Its brick spandrels and continuous wraparound windows elicit vistas up and down the Hudson and make this a modernist landmark well worth the trek out west. A few years ago the building saw an influx, followed by a rapid outflux, of dot-commers. Among the current inhabitants are Martha Stewart's studio, the late Jay Chiat's Screaming Media, and several noteworthy art galleries and a rare bookstore. An elevator, originally used to hoist freight-train cars and now used by FedEx trucks, can be found at the building's core.

DESIGN WORKS
6 Henry Urbach Architecture
526 West 26th Street

An architect by training, Urbach aims with his gallery to create "a laboratory for investigations into the nature and potential of contemporary space." These investigations have resulted in exhibits of Richard Barnes's photographs of Ted Kaczynski's cabin, and the dream-state renderings of experimental architect Lebbeus Woods. Among the experimental architectural studios that Urbach represents are Diller + Scofidio and LOT/EK, who designed the space.

ART DISTRICT PIONEER
7 Matthew Marks Gallery
523 West 24th Street

Marks was the Chelsea art district's primary pioneer. In 1994 he moved his gallery from an apartment space on Madison Avenue to an ambulance garage on a windswept and (apart from the cab drivers washing their cars) deserted 22nd Street. Now he shares with Barbara Gladstone a disused knife factory on 24th Street, and his artists include Nan Goldin, Gary Hume, Fischli/Weiss, Roni Horn and Andreas Gursky.

MINIMAL GALLERY
8 Luhring Augustine
531 West 24th Street

This minimal gallery – another Gluckman design – was founded in 1985 by co-owners Lawrence R. Luhring and Roland J. Augustine. Check out the imposing back office where the big deals are made. The gallery's critical monographic exhibitions of Marcel Duchamp, Gerhard Richter and Donald Judd put it firmly on the map. And it continues to show German painters like Gunther Forg and Sigmar Polke, along with international photographers and conceptual artists – Sophie Calle, Robert Gober and Rachel Whiteread among them.

PORT OUT, STARBOARD HOME
9 The Maritime Hotel
118

UPTOWN BARGAINS DOWNTOWN
10 Barneys Co-op
162

WHOLESALE FINE FOOD
11 Chelsea Market
75 Ninth Avenue

Originally the Nabisco factory and the birthplace of America's best-loved cookie, the Oreo, this building is today a buzzing market complex. Its street-block-sized interior houses a variety of specialty food shops that double as wholesale and retail outlets. Architect Jeff Vandeberg and developer Irwin Cohen have created a playful atmosphere using features from the original factory, such as gears, pipes and machines, as sculptural details along the central concourse.

After an evening of hopping from gallery-opening to gallery-opening, curators, artists and dealers flock to the Chelsea art scene's favorite feeding ground. The delicious Tuscan food satisfies the body, leaving the mind to ponder such critical issues as the future of landscape painting in contemporary art practice. Fifteen wines are offered by the glass to accompany dishes such as bocconcini of fresh mozzarella, tuna carpaccio and bresaola with arugula. At lunchtime ask for a table on the patio seating area, one of the finest outdoor oases in town.

Printed Matter, Inc. is the world's largest non-profit institution dedicated to the promotion of publications made by artists in a book-like format. After many years of operation in SoHo, Printed Matter moved its stock – limited-edition artworks, books, magazines and objects that blur both the definitions of and the boundaries between books and art – to new, larger premises in the heart of the Chelsea art district. While the store still maintains its roots in traditional artists' books by the likes of Sol LeWitt, Lawrence Weiner and Ed Ruscha, it has recently begun to explore more contemporary interpretations of the genre, including video tapes, CD-ROMS, multiples, along with exhibition catalogs and monographs.

14 Max Protetch Gallery

511 West 22nd Street

In addition to casting his net beyond the conventional boundary of art practice, Protetch specializes in drawings by architects. Since 1978, when he moved his gallery from Washington to New York, he has shown the work of Robert Venturi, Michael Graves, Zaha Hadid, Frank Gehry and Tadao Ando. The gallery represents the estates of Frank Lloyd Wright and Buckminster Fuller, and also has on its books such artists as Oliver Herring, David Reed, Thomas Nozkowski, Byron Kim, Iñigo Manglano-Ovalle and João Penalva. A recent show by Manglano filled the gallery with a fiberglass-and-titanium-alloy-foil scale model of a 20-mile-long (30-kilometer) cumulonimbus cloud entitled *Cloud Prototype No. 1, 2003.*

15 DIA Center for the Arts

545 and 548 West 22nd Street

Take the elevator to the roof of this Gluckman Mayner-renovated building and start your visit with a bitter espresso in the small café you'll find there. Enter the Dan Graham "Rooftop Urban Park Project" glass sculpture and rotate 360 degrees, taking in the view of boats coming down the Hudson River, the immediate skyline of water towers and local gallerists' rooftop terraces. Then descend the staircase lined with Dan Flavin's fluorescent light pieces, floor by floor, viewing the large, long-running exhibitions of works by such artists as Lawrence Weiner, Ann Hamilton and Fred Sandback. Leave some time for browsing the playful ground-level bookstore with its tiled floor in boiled-sweet hues designed by Cuban artist Jorge Pardo.

FASHION MOTHERSHIP
16 Comme des Garçons
520 West 22nd Street

With an entrance that looks like the gangplank to an alien spacecraft, it's hard to resist the lure of this veritable gallery of a shop, an appropriate environment for the structural architectonics of Rei Kawakubo's cult line of clothing. Future Systems, the experimental British firm that designed the space in 1998, kept the building's 19th-century façade intact and focused instead on creating the asymmetric tubular entrance made from aluminum.

A WORLD OF TEA
17 Wild Lily Tearoom
511A West 22nd Street

Take a break from art viewing and soothe your over-stimulated synapses with a nice cup of tea. Choose from a menu of more than 40 connoisseur-grade teas – from China, India, Taiwan and Japan – at this peaceful sanctuary designed by David Hu. You can sip your Tong Tin Oolong and nibble delicate Japanese sandwiches beside a small pond containing lily pads and four large goldfish.

CLEAN AND SIMPLE
18 Malin + Goetz
177 Seventh Avenue

New York duo Matthew Malin and Andrew Goetz created a unisex skincare system that consists of just six items: one cleanser and one moisturizer each for face, hair and body. Craig Konyk's minimalist store design set the tone for the packaging, designed by New York firm 2x4 in a limited palette of blue, green, red and all-caps Helvetica. And lest the whole thing sounds too sharp and clean, the shop dogs Bob and Junior are on hand, lounging in the window, to mess things up a bit.

ECCENTRIC TAPAS
19 El Quijote
226 West 23rd Street

This 60-year-old Spanish restaurant is the cafeteria – albeit one serving lobster and paella – for eccentric guests of the Chelsea hotel. The reason to stay, though, is the bar, which provides old-fashioned drinks, a comprehensive catalog of Quijote figurines, and a vantage point over the dining room with its red banquettes filled with fascinating parties. Spend at least part of an evening propped up at this bar, savoring the musty aura of an old New York where waiters wear uniforms and bow ties, and the fur- and fedora-wearing clientele still Brylcreem their hair and smoke cigarettes from silver cases.

PARKING-LOT-SIZED BAR
20 Lot 61
550 West 21st Street

This enormous loft bar and restaurant, designed by architect Rafael Viñoly, was one of the first to install site-specific art works. With a nod to the gallery district that it feeds and waters, Lot 61 spotted its interior with Damien Hirst, bedecked its ceilings with Jorge Pardo's hanging cylindrical lamps, and announced its restrooms with Jim Hodge's fluorescent "Hello" light.

"I REMEMBER YOU WELL"
21 Hotel Chelsea

ART OF DISCO
22 Passerby

ART SMART
23 Scalo
436 West 15th Street

This Swiss combination of a publishing firm and gallery for photography, art and popular culture now has a project space formerly occupied by Gavin Brown's Enterprise (p. 17), and next door to the still fabulous Passerby bar.

BURGERS A GO-GO
24 Pop Burger
58–60 Ninth Avenue

In need of a quick post-gallery-viewing or pre-shopping snack? Pop Burger serves fries, onion rings and itty-bitty burgers at a no-frills, brightly-lit lunch counter. For a more leisurely meal, come in the evening and take a seat in the lounge area at the back. Pop Burger, the latest collaborative venture of restaurateur Roy Liebenthal and designer Ali Tayar, has survived the initial hype onslaught and celebrity showings and is now safe to pop into.

ROOFTOP SPLENDOR
25 Hotel Gansevoort

The Red Cat's menu reflects the warmth and comfort of the restaurant's ambience with unpretentious, well-executed American bistro dishes. If you do not feel like making the commitment to a shell steak with Yukon golds, fennel and aïoli with Cabernet sauce, then order some sides – particularly the parmesan French fries and red-hot rapini – to eat with a glass of excellent wine at the bar. The red-and-white barnwood interior has a New England feel, but the addition of huge hanging candle lanterns from Morocco saves it from cute pastiche.

La Lunchonette's friendly, slightly dishevelled interior is an inviting oasis and a welcome contrast to the desolate street it has inhabited since 1988. Chef Jean-François Fraysse and his wife, Melva Max, jointly own the place and serve up delicious French dishes such as lamb sausage with sautéed apples and pan-fried whole trout with wild mushrooms. On Sundays the restaurant features live jazz.

DJ Nicolas Matar runs a club with less attitude and more ambience than many of his competitors in the Meatpacking District. Inspired by the atmosphere of late 1980s New York nightlife, Matar focuses on the music above all else. As you'd expect of a former resident at Pacha in Ibiza, Matar's staple fare is house music, but at Cielo, it's eclectic, worldly and soulful enough to be interesting. Stephane Dupoux has surrounded the sunken dance-floor with brown and beige suede banquettes, and enhanced the 1970s aesthetic with lighting effects.

18

PARISIAN BISTRO

30 Pastis

9 Ninth Avenue

Even though you know this is a pitch-perfect simulation, a Disneyfication of a Parisian bistro, there are moments (on a weekday morning, for example) when – with an espresso, a newspaper plucked from the rack just inside the door, and a sunlit breakfast spread out on your window-side table – it feels great. Restaurateur Keith McNally, whose other restaurants include Lucky Strike, Pravda and Balthazar (p. 22), has surpassed himself with attention to detail in his conversion of a wholesale flower market into Pastis. Chefs Riad Nasr and Lee Hanson serve dishes inspired by hearty Provençal cuisine. Avoid the late-night invasion of uptowners and out-of-towners slumming it in the Meatpacking District, and limit yourself to daytime and early evening visits.

MEAT MARKET CHIC

31 Meet

71–73 Gansevoort Street

Feng-shui master Tin Sun acted as consultant on design, construction and placement of elements in this transformation of a meat freezer into a modern-day meat market for the chic and sleek. The communal handbasin in the bathroom is a 140-pound (64-kg), 1-inch-thick (4-cm) slab of amber onyx mounted on a steel frame with stainless-steel taps affixed to a mirrored wall. Back in the restaurant, a central, inclining catwalk of coconut wood divides the large space into two different dining levels, each filled with polished rattan chairs and cream-colored, ostrich-leather banquettes.

MOD COVETABLES

32 Auto

167

SASSY DINER
33 Florent
69 Gansevoort Street

Florent, a diner that has been serving 24 hours of attitude a day since 1985, was given its graphic and visual form by the late Tibor Kalman of New York's famously irreverent design company M&Co. Come to this fluorescent-lit diner to talk politics, bounce wisecracks back and forth with the transsexual waitresses, and, if you are a local, to open your mail with a mug of coffee at the Formica counter. Florent's forcefully liberal views on the changes in the neighborhood and the world are expressed with witty succinctness in white letters on a menu board. The food is inexpensive French bistro fare, like French onion soup, boudin noir and goat-cheese salad.

ALADDIN'S CAVE OF SHOES
34 Jeffrey
449 West 14th Street

When Jeffrey first opened on the far west reaches of 14th Street in 1999, there were precious few other shops in the Meatpacking District. Taxicabs would emit fur-clad and Manolo-shod ladies who had to gingerly make their way past skinned carcasses swinging from the doorways of meat lockers to get to the mini-department store's front door. Today the contrasts are less stark and the gasps are reserved solely for the dazzling footwear displays – Jeffrey Kalinsky, the store's owner, was a former shoe buyer at Barneys.

FURNITURE FOR WORK AND PLAY
35 Vitra Showroom
29 Ninth Avenue

These offices and showroom for the furniture company Vitra were designed by architect-of-the-moment Lindy Roy. Her conversion of a turn-of-the-20th-century storage space is a study of sensual modernism. Three stories are connected by two slots that incorporate staircases, and large rubber-wrapped display surfaces that extend the floor area of the second-floor showroom down into the retail space and gallery below.

PRETTY DRESSES
36 Lucy Barnes
320 West 14th Street

Embroidery, hand stitching, beading, sequins, diaphanous flowers, appliqués and ruched silk are inspirations for and delightful features of Lucy Barnes's girlie garments. Her other eponymous store on Perry Street carries vintage pieces to complement her contemporary collections of both ready-to-wear and custom-made creations.

CUPCAKE HEAVEN
37 Magnolia Bakery
401 Bleecker Street

The cupcakes under 1950s bell jars in the window of this chaotic, old-fashioned bakeshop are what devotees travel from all over town for. Pink, yellow and brown butter icing is slapped inches-thick on to the palm-sized sponge cakes and then topped with lurid sprinkles. You can take them away in boxes for parties, but most people choose to linger with their prize in the sugary steam of the café or on the small bench outside.

"WE LOVE MARC JACOBS"
38 Marc Jacobs
172

IT'S A WRAP
39 Diane von Furstenberg
385 West 12th Street

For Diane von Furstenberg's classically sexy silk jersey wrap dresses in her signature prints and solid colors, head to her shimmering store in the far reaches of the West Village. The wraps, along with ruched tops, slim-fitting, ultra-suede trousers, and coordinating accessories, are presented in a space designed by BE Partners and Bill Katz.

The wall and ceiling treatment consists of plaster spotted with flush, 4-inch (10-cm) mirror disks and halogen lamps. The dressing rooms, in the center of the store, are enclosed in a circle of ceiling-to-floor white silk draperies and the Furstenberg dotted logo is deployed on sandblasted-glass pivot doors that separate the retail and event spaces.

TRAVEL KIT
40 Flight 001
96 Greenwich Avenue

Brad John and John Sencion have cornered the *Wallpaper**-toting, wanderlust market with their mod West Village travel boutique. For real adventurers there are travel guides, leather passport holders, backpacks, wash bags and Braun travel clocks. For the more armchair inclined, there are globes, retro watches and coffee-table books. Dario C. Antonio's design for the store includes rubber flooring, a glowing back wall, and universal travel symbols in powder blue for decorative detail.

BEER AND BURGERS
41 Corner Bistro
140

OLD-FASHIONED DELIGHTS
42 Li-Lac Chocolates
120 Christopher Street

With 5,000 moulds in all shapes and sizes, the chocolatiers at this tiny, ribbon-tied box of a shop are ready to make your chocolate fantasies come true. Established by a French family in the 1920s, Li-Lac Chocolates has been in the same 1883 building ever since. It's a favorite destination for the Villagers, despite long lines during holidays.

GAS-LIT PHARMACY
43 C.O. Bigelow Apothecaries
414 Sixth Avenue

This 162-year-old apothecary is still outfitted with its original 1838 wood shelving, tiles, ceiling mouldings and gas chandeliers. Old Delftware drug jars and historic prescriptions are interspersed with Bigelow's merchandise, which encompasses an in-house line of perfumed oils, its Alchemy line of make-up, and old American standards, such as Calgon and Ivory. Illustrious former customers include Samuel L. Clemens, better known as Mark Twain, who lived around the corner at 21 Fifth Avenue.

Gramercy Park
East Village
Lower East Side
Lower Manhattan

This exploration of the eastern flank of Manhattan begins at the island's well-fed right thigh and ends at its en pointe toe. In historical terms the journey runs counter to the city's evolution. Beginning with the once-far-uptown settlement of Gramercy Square, where the wealthiest knickerbockers congregated, it continues through the slums of the immigrant staging posts of the Lower East Side and finally arrives in the oldest part of New York, which was, from 1626 until it overcrowded in the mid-19th century, New York's chaotic center.

Gramercy Park is the centerpiece of a historic district of tree-shaded streets lined with a variety of 19th-century residences, from 1840s row houses and brownstones to Victorian-era Queen Annes and neo-Gothics, which lend the area a particular gentility.

The East Village's history starts circa 1960 when it branched off from the Lower East Side as an area self-defined by its countercultural activity centered on a few coffee houses and clubs around St. Mark's Place. The area was plagued with drug-related crime throughout the 1970s and 1980s and provided the gritty backdrop for an exciting art and punk-rock scene. The Giuliani-administered clean-up of Tompkins Square Park in 1992 brought a trail of French bistros and media types in its wake, pushing its original residents and those who arrived too late to the southeast. These pioneers found themselves in a Lower East Side both stained and bespangled by its longstanding role as the immigrant gateway for the rest of New York. The first wave of arrivals took place throughout the 19th century, when political events in Europe and anti-Chinese sentiment on the West Coast fanned the sails of boatloads of settlers towards New York. A century later, in the 1960s, following a relaxation of immigration laws, streams of new colors, languages, religions and cultures formed vibrant and sometimes violent eddies in the area. The most recent flood of new blood is largely Puerto Rican, Dominican and young white musicians and artists. Ludlow and Orchard were the scenes of a severe attack of hipification in the 1990s, and Clinton and Rivington are the ongoing sites of more recent and, thankfully, more considered creative intrusion.

Continuing south and further back in time you arrive at the narrow, tangled streets laid out by 17th-century Dutch settlers, when the city was still known as New Amsterdam. Among the closely packed top-heavy financial and Old World corporate centers and smoky, back-alley taverns down the crooked lanes that resisted the imposition of the 19th-century grid, it's easy to lose your sense of time and space — that is, until you emerge into the southernmost territory of the island, where a boat ride or walk across the Brooklyn Bridge provides an exhilarating view of the city.

360-DEGREE DESIGN

1   Hotel on Rivington

GOTHIC ARCHITECTURE, MEMBERS ONLY

2   National Arts Club

15 Gramercy Park South

Built in 1845, this building has housed the National Arts Club and its members – the first of whom included Theodore Roosevelt and Woodrow Wilson – since 1906. Its original flat-front, iron-grilled appearance matched the style of the houses still maintained on the west side of Gramercy Park. But in the 1880s the mansion's owner, Samuel Tilden, hired Calvert Vaux – one of the designers of Central Park – to bring the façade up to tempo with the current trend for High Victorian style. Vaux duly added bay windows, polychromatic brickwork and Gothic ornamentation. During exhibitions and events when the public is admitted, you can see the stained-glass ceilings that John LaFarge created for the inside of the mansion and the Italian carved fireplaces. You may even see Martin Scorsese, Ethan Hawke, Dennis Hopper and Uma Thurman, who are among the club's current members.

SALADS AND DOUBLE-CHOCOLATE COOKIES

3   City Bakery

3 West 18th Street

Visit City Bakery for a sublime chocolate experience that might include a "shot" of viscous dark chocolate scooped from a constantly churning vat, or a huge double-chocolate cookie freshly baked by pastry chef and owner, Maury Rubin. For lunch, this airy café, frequented by designers and photographers from the surrounding Flatiron district, has the best seasonal salad counter in town, assembled by chef Ilene Rosen. The bakery holds bizarre food festivals throughout the year, such as the "City Bakery State Fair" in July when the otherwise urbane space undergoes a country makeover with a carpet of hay, a picket fence and gingham-clad girls serving corn dogs and lemonade.

ALE AND WINGS SINCE 1864

4   Pete's Tavern

129 East 18th Street

The heart of Irving Place is an Irish saloon that has been serving "grocery and grog" since 1864. It even stayed open during Prohibition, disguised as a flower shop. Popular legend has it that one of the regulars, O. Henry, wrote his 1902 classic *Gift of the Magi* at the first booth by the door.

Today the bar has an Italian-American menu, three TV screens and a loyal crowd of after-work drinkers. Pete's own 1864 Original Ale is still drawn from old porcelain taps set in the 30-foot-long (9-meter) rosewood bar.

NEW AMERICAN DIY

5   Craft

A GOURMET COUNTRY REFUGE

6   Gramercy Tavern

42 East 20th Street

For some New American gastronomic indulgence, consider Tom Colicchio's market menu at the well-established and well-loved Gramercy Tavern. It involves a taste of almost everything on the exceptional menu and reaches a crescendo with three of Claudia Fleming's wonderful desserts, possibly including a mascarpone cream Napoleon with rhubarb compote and strawberries. For a less expensive alternative there is the handsome bar in the festive Tavern Room at the front of the rustic-themed restaurant. With more than 85 selections, the cheese course ranks as one of the city's finest. Order a selection of three, six or ten as a dessert, or sample with wine at the bar. The service throughout is impeccable; service staff tell you how dishes taste, not just what's in them.

WHARTONESQUE RETREAT

7   The Inn at Irving Place

INDIAN-INFUSED CUISINE

8   Tabla

11 Madison Avenue

Young Bombay-born chef Floyd Cardoz fuses American and Indian cuisines at this flamboyantly designed restaurant in the Art Déco Metropolitan Life Tower. Dishes such as tandoori quail with black-pepper glaze, taro-dusted halibut with white beans, and scallops in mustard-oil-red-pepper coulis have earned Cardoz the adoring attention of New York food critics. The richly colored, curvy space features a suspended second floor around a "viewing well." Here you can snack on grape-pine-nut and tomato-kalonji chutneys or guacamole with toasted cumin on a variety of breads. The restaurant's owner is Danny Meyer, whose other smash successes are Union Square Café, Gramercy Tavern and Eleven Madison Park. For a taste of his style to go, try a gourmet-prepared hot dog from the shake shack located in the southeast corner of Madison Square Park.

9 Greenmarket
Union Square, East 17th Street and Broadway

Before ducking underground to catch the L train to Williamsburg (only two stops away), savor the smells and colors of the farmers' produce stalls that cluster at the northern end of Union Square. Dating from 1839, the square has been a traditional platform for political rallies and labor protests. The few remaining radicals now share the steps and railings with skateboarding tricksters and breakdancers, watched by yuppies having their lunch in the sunshine. The market is open Monday, Wednesday, Friday and Saturday.

NO-FRILLS BEAUTY PRODUCTS
10 Kiehl's

DELICIOUS DESSERT BAR
11 ChiKaLicious
203 East 10th Street

This intimate, 20–seat bôite is built around an open kitchen where chefs Don and Chika Tillman and Donna Ryan work and serve customers directly. There is a three-course prix-fixe menu for $12, beginning with an amuse bouche of kiwi marinated in lavender soup with yogurt sorbet, followed by such "main courses" as Toasted Earl Grey Tea Brioche with Candied Kumquats and Vanilla Sorbet. Recommended wines are listed with each choice of menu.

BOOKMARK
12 St. Mark's Bookshop
31 Third Avenue

Established in 1977, St. Mark's bookstore is one of the last vestiges of the legendary East Village intellectual scene. Open until midnight every day of the week, the store is just as much a hangout spot for students, academics and arts professionals as it is a repository of specialist books and periodicals. St. Mark's specialties include cultural theory, graphic design, poetry and film studies, as well as stock from small press publishers.

CLANDESTINE COCKTAILS
13 Angel's Share
156

JAPANESE NETHERWORLD

14 Decibel
240 East 9th Street

From the moment you descend the steps and ring the buzzer for this basement bar you're submerged in a Japanese netherworld. Low lighting, an idiosyncratic soundtrack and kooky Japanese bar staff combine to create an atmosphere that can vary from subdued to wild in the space of one evening. The wooden bar in the front room conceals a den in the back for some seated sake and appetizer consumption. The okonomiyaki (Japanese pancake) is a house favorite.

BEER, SPIT AND SAWDUST

15 McSorley's Old Ale House
151

DINING ON THE HALF-SHELL

16 Jack's Luxury Oyster Bar
144

INDIAN-SPICED FABRICS

17 Alpana Bawa
70 East 1st Street

Punjab-born Alpana Bawa threads her Indian heritage into the fabric of her vividly colored and immaculately tailored clothing line. Her original construction methods and use of color have earned her "darling" status among fashion critics. Beaded evening gowns and pink and lilac tanks embroidered with leaves and vines are among the favorites of her female fans. Men, too, can strut their funky stuff in architecturally inspired shirts.

URBAN PASTORAL

18 Community Garden
East 6th Street and Avenue B

Where once a garbage- and weed-filled lot stood at the corner of East 6th Street and Avenue B, there now thrives a lush and magical community garden, replete with wisteria-creeping arbors. A 37-foot (11-meter) tower built by a lifelong neighborhood resident from material discarded by local people is the centerpiece of the garden's cultivated plots and shady paths. The garden, both the quirkiest and prettiest of the many fenced-in patches of land planted with trees, bushes and flower beds in the Lower East Side, is open to the public on Saturday and Sunday afternoons.

CAVIAR AND PICKLES

19 Russ & Daughters

179 East Houston Street

Joel Russ began serving schmaltz herring in a barrel and salt-cured lox at this location in the 1920s. His daughters – Hattie, Ida and Anne – joined him at the spotless white-tiled counter in the 1940s. Now in its fourth generation of ownership, the delicatessen, which the Smithsonian Institution deems to be "part of New York's cultural heritage," is still going strong. People come from all over the city for gleaming beluga, osetra and sevruga caviar, smoked sturgeon, herring and salmon, as well as candied fruits and nuts. Just outside the door, you can check the time by the scrambled numbers on the clock on top of the Red Square apartment building, designed by Tibor Kalman.

I'LL HAVE WHAT SHE'S HAVING

20 Katz's Delicatessen

145

COMFORT FOOD

21 Freeman's

137

MOBY'S TEASHOP

22 Teany

150

CANDIES GALORE

23 Economy Candy

108 Rivington Street

This cluttered candy warehouse has been selling jawbreakers, strawberry shoelaces and Atomic Fireballs a penny a piece since 1937. The store's owner, Jerry Cohen, will climb a ladder to reach your favorite jar from the floor-to-ceiling shelves.

BISTRO DINING

24 Schiller's Liquor Bar

131 Rivington Street

Some of the interior details at Schiller's, such as the white-tiled walls, hint at the site's previous incarnation as a pharmacy. As is often the case with New York's trendier restaurants, mornings and lunchtimes are best. Order a couple of freshly made dollar doughnuts to munch while you wait with your newspapers for a breakfast of eggs hussard, or sour cream and hazelnut waffles served with mixed berries and bourbon maple syrup.

25 TG170
170 Ludlow Street

Terry Gillis has launched many a fashion career from her pioneering store at 170 Ludlow. Her labels of choice include Pixie Yates, Living Doll, United Bamboo, Ulla Johnson and Liz Collins. Accessories include bags that range from the messenger functionality of Freitag, to the delicate whimsy of purses made from vintage kimono fabric. In the T-shirt department is Supersonic's hot-dog-print muscle-tee, in addition to perennial favorites from Petit Bateau.

IMMIGRANT LIFE
26 Lower East Side Tenement Museum
90 Orchard Street

Made up of a series of tenement buildings and accessible by guided tour only, this fascinating museum explores the experiences of immigrants in the late 19th century. The Lower East Side is referred to as the "gateway to America" for the vast number of immigrants it has housed (often in appalling conditions) over the years. This tenement at 90 Orchard, for example, was home to an estimated 7,000 people from more than 20 nations between 1863 and 1935. It is now carefully restored to allow a glimpse into the lives of actual residents from different historical periods.

ROMANTIC GERMAN SYNAGOGUE
27 Angel Orensanz Foundation
172 Norfolk Street

This synagogue was commissioned from architect Alexander Seltzer in 1849 by members of the German Jewish community, who arrived in Manhattan in the 1840s. In 1986 the sculptor Angel Orensanz bought the decaying building and saved it from demolition. Now the neo-Gothic space, with its 50-foot-high (15-meter) ceilings, is rented out for candle-lit parties and cultural events such as Alexander McQueen's first American show and Rainer Werner Fassbinder's *City, Garbage and Death*.

GOURMAND'S STRIP
28 Clinton Street
- 71 Clinton Fresh Food, no. 71
- aka Café, no. 49
- WD–50, no. 50

When they set up their restaurant on a deserted stretch of Clinton Street in 1999, owners Dewey Dufresne and Janet Nelson thought they would be "opening a restaurant that would be moderately priced and have a nice local atmosphere." Thanks to a combination of the restaurant's contemporary design (exposed brick, vinyl banquettes and orange and green walls on the inside and an aluminum and glass frontage), the "hipification" of Clinton Street, and the stunning creations of chef Willie Dufresne, it shot right out of the "neighborhood" category into the island-wide stratosphere. Today, although Dufresne cooks at his own restaurant, WD-50, right across the road in a converted bodega, and has left No. 71 in the hands of Jason Neroni, many of his original creations are still on the menu. The goat-cheese tart topped with sliced potatoes and dotted with rich applewood-smoked bacon, still stuns the critics. Soups, sandwiches and empanadas are the staples of aka Café, No.71's smaller, more casual offshoot, just a couple of doors up the street.

GOOD LIBATIONS
29 Good World Barber Shop
150

CHINA ON THE CHEAP
30 Dumpling House
118a Eldridge Street

If you long for the alleys of Beijing, visit this hole-in-the-wall dumpling house where the food — and the prices — are absolutely authentic. Feast on five pork-and-chive dumplings for one dollar, and add a sesame pancake to mop up the hot sauce for another fifty cents. Once a closely guarded secret, the word is now out. While you wait in line for your Styrofoam take-out container, owner Vanessa Duan and staff prepare your food over steaming pans and spitting skillets.

DOUGHNUTS, DAHLING!
31 Doughnut Plant
379 Grand Street

From the street you can observe the inner workings of this Roald Dahl-esque factory as it produces an eye-popping selection of enormous hand-glazed doughnuts. The colorful confections are baked to an old Lower East Side family recipe that has been passed down to current proprietor, Mark Isreal. The list of choices is long and ever-changing, to include seasonally inspired varieties like pumpkin, nostalgic ones like malted milk, and the perennially delicious Valrhona-Chocolate.

32 Brown + Orange
61 Hester Street

Mexican-born surfer/chef Alejandro Alcocer converted this tiny, gallery space into a café ostensibly to provide good coffee to an espresso-deprived neighborhood. He also brought in good simple foods, such as French cheese and raisin-walnut bread, sourced during a decade of global travel prior to settling in the Lower East Side. These items are sold at Orange, the delicatessen half of the enterprise. Regular brunchers at Brown recommend the Tuscan breakfast platter.

REGGAE RAPTURE
33 Deadly Dragon Sound System
102b Forsyth Street

After three years of causing a ruckus in Chicago's reggae community, in 1998 Deadly Dragon Sound System moved to New York. With more than 150,000 pieces of vinyl and acetate in its vaults, ranging from classic Ska numbers to more contemporary interpretations, this store is a prized resource for reggae browsers and fanatics alike.

MONEY TEMPLE
34 New York Stock Exchange
8 Broad Street

Built in 1903 by George B. Post, this marble temple's two-story base and Corinthian columns signify permanence and power. Although visitors are currently not able to view the frenetic trading floor, the Exchange is an appropriate starting point for an exploration into the district's fusion of finance and power-architecture. The Museum of American Financial History (24 Broadway) tells the history of Wall Street through displays of ancient ticker-tape machines, telegraphs and trading tables. If you book well ahead, you can also visit the Federal Reserve Bank of New York (33 Liberty Street), which holds the nation's largest store of gold. The limestone-clad skyscraper of Bank of New York (1 Wall Street and Broadway) was built in 1932 and its banking hall is an Art Déco feast of gold, orange and red mosaic tiles.

HIGH-RISE HISTORIES
35 Skyscraper Museum
39 Battery Place

At the base of the Ritz Carlton Hotel in Battery Park, the long-migratory Skyscraper Museum has found a permanent home. Designed by skyscraper titans Skidmore, Owings & Merrill, the facility contains one gallery devoted to the evolution of New York's commercial skyline, and another to changing shows that explore aspects of high-rise building. An after-museum cocktail in the hotel's 14th-floor Rise bar affords clear views across the harbor to the Statue of Liberty. Alternatively, a sea-breezy walk across Battery Park takes you to the Staten Island Ferry terminal. From here you can ride to and from Staten Island (about 30 minutes each way) taking in close-up views of Alexandre Gustave Eiffel's Statue of Liberty on the way out, and on the return, a southerly perspective of the high rises of Lower Manhattan, all for no charge.

ROMANCING THE BRIDGE
36 Brooklyn Bridge and Bridge Café
279 Water Street

A decorative pressed-tin ceiling, ample windows displaying the Manhattan-bound arches of the Brooklyn Bridge, and a setting in one of the city's oldest food-service buildings are just a few features that make the delightfully snug and (in the evening) positively romantic Bridge Café worth a visit. Once sated, walk the pedestrian platform that traverses the outer edge of Brooklyn Bridge, that lyrical 1883 construction of soaring steel-wire cables and neo-Gothic towers that was at one time the largest suspension bridge in the world and the first to be constructed in steel. On the far side is Brooklyn Heights, a small enclave of early- and mid-19th-century brownstones and brick houses, once the homes of prosperous ship captains and now populated by wealthy filmmakers and stockbrokers. Stroll the Brooklyn Heights Promenade between Cranberry and Remsen Streets for a view of Lower Manhattan's skyline, especially magical at sunset.

A COLONIAL INN
37 Fraunces Tavern
54 Pearl Street

In the final days of the Revolutionary War, Fraunces Tavern served as George Washington's residence, and it was in the Long Room that he delivered his farewell to the officers of the Continental army on December 4, 1783 before returning to his residence at Mount Vernon. In 1904 the historic significance of the then-decaying building was realized, and it was reconstructed to look like a late 18th-century inn. Today Wall Street traders frequent the colonial-style street-level dining room, and there is a museum on the upper floors, if a little dusty, that has a certain charm.

join our
mailing list
for tasting,
special
events &
new
products

ORANGE
EPICERIE

Midtown

Approximate scale

1/2 kilometer

1/4 mile

Central Park

Central
Park
Zoo

The Pond

**LENOX
HILL**

Columbus
Circle

Central Park South

West 58th Street

West 57th Street

West 56th Street

West 55th Street

West 54th Street

West 53rd Street

West 52nd Street

West 51st Street

West 50th Street

West 49th Street

West 48th Street

West 47th Street

West 46th Street

West 45th Street

West 44th Street

West 43rd Street

West 42nd Street

West 41st Street

West 40th Street

West 39th Street

West 38th Street

West 37th Street

West 36th Street

MIDTOWN

Radio City
Music Hall

Rockefeller Plaza

Rockefeller
Center

Times
Square

Port
Authority
Bus
Terminal

Bryant
Park

New York
Public
Library
7

**GARMENT
DISTRICT**

Eighth Avenue

Broadway

Seventh Avenue

Sixth Avenue

Fifth Avenue

Madison Avenue

Vanderbilt Avenue

Park Avenue

Depew Place

Lexington Avenue

Third Avenue

Second Avenue

First Avenue

York Avenue

Franklin D. Roosevelt Drive

East 73rd Street

East 72nd Street

East 70th Street

East 70th Street

East 69th Street

East 68th Street

East 67th Street

East 66th Street

East 65th Street

East 64th Street

East 63rd Street

East 62nd Street

East 61st Street

East 60th Street

Queensbo

East 59th Street

East 59th Street

East 58th Street

East 57th Street

East 56th Street

East 55th Street

East 54th St

East 53rd Street

East 52nd St

East 51st St

East 50th St

East 49th St

East 48th St

East 47th St

East 46th St

East 45th St

East 44th St

East 43rd St

East 42nd Street

East 41st Street

East 40th Street

East 39th St

East 38th St

East 37th St

East 36th St

**TURTLE
BAY**

Sutton Place

Seagram
Building

Grand
Central
Station
2
3

Chrysler
Building
8

United Nations
Headquarters
9

Queens - Midtown T

Tunnel Exit Street

Franklin D. Roosevelt Drive

**MURRAY
HILL**

Pierpont
Morgan
Library
1

29

17

19 **18**

12

20

13

22

28

24   **5**
          6

4

11

16

10
15

14

26 **27**

31

23

32

21 **30**

25

Midtown is New York at its most vertiginous and luminous. On street level, the traffic lights turn and the crowds cross the grids like clockwork. Overhead, the lofty ambitions of mid-century Modernist architecture reach towards infinity. From broad-shouldered corporate headquarters along the "Park Avenue Corridor" to the designer flagships of Fifth Avenue, and from the fiber-optic stars that twinkle on the ceiling of Grand Central Station to the diode-cacophony of Times Square, Midtown condenses and amplifies the energy of the city in ways that are both exhausting and exhilarating.

Among the pillars of commerce are some pioneers of 1950s "glass box" architecture, including the Seagram Building by Mies van der Rohe and Philip Johnson, and the newly restored Lever House by Skidmore, Owings & Merrill (SOM), which was the city's first building to be constructed entirely from steel and glass. The postmodern response came in the improbable forms of Philip Johnson's "Lipstick Building," Edward Barnes's black granite prism for IBM and Johnson's Chippendale breakfront top for AT&T (now owned by Sony).

Grand Central Station, designed in 1913 and newly emerged from a decade-long renovation program, combines an extraordinary feat of urban planning — multilevel circulation for cars, trains, subways and pedestrians — and magnificent Beaux Arts architecture. The terminal was preserved after many years of decline, thanks to a campaign spearheaded by Jacqueline Onassis. The romantic revival Pennsylvania Station further southwest of Grand Central was not so lucky. The 1910 building, a noble gateway to the city, designed by McKim, Mead & White, was unceremoniously torn down in the 1960s and replaced by a nondescript cat-flap of an entryway. Now, the General Post Office across the street is being transformed by SOM into a new Penn Station with a soaring arch of steel and glass.

In the mid- to late-19th century, Midtown was the most fashionable residential neighborhood in New York. The Vanderbilts alone had four mansions between 34th and 59th Streets. Today, little remains of this genteel past except for the two exquisite buildings that now house Cartier and Versace. The new occupants of Fifth Avenue are flagship shops — Tiffany, Calvin Klein, Gucci — and upmarket department stores — Henri Bendel, Bergdorf Goodman, Barneys — emitting their distilled essences via the streams of branded shopping bags that flow up and down the thoroughfare. Midtown is also the center of the city's media and publishing industries. At the power-lunch hour, when television, magazine and web executives sally out to Michael's or The Four Seasons, the river of shopping totes absorbs tributaries of briefcases and laptop cases from which protrude furled copies of *The New York Times*, *The New Yorker* or *Harper's*.

1 The Morgan Library

29 East 36th Street

By 1906, J. Pierpont Morgan, banker, philanthropist and collector, needed a building in which to house his amazing collection of rare books, Old Master drawings and autographed manuscripts. Charles McKim gave him an Italian Renaissance-style palazzo with three magnificent rooms epitomizing America's Age of Elegance. Among the highlights of the library, located in Murray Hill, are three copies of the Gutenberg Bible, Charles Dickens's manuscript of *A Christmas Carol*, Henry David Thoreau's journals and Thomas Jefferson's letters to his daughter Martha. There is a pleasant courtyard café, but if you're in the mood for something stronger, duck down into the dark hideaway of the Andrée Putman-designed Morgans Bar, beneath Morgans Hotel at 237 Madison Avenue and 37th Street.

MONUMENT TO MOVEMENT

2 Grand Central Station

42nd Street

While this 1913 Beaux Arts terminal is a thrilling point of departure for a train journey, there's plenty to do here without buying a ticket. Spend a while observing the 300,000 commuters bend deftly around obstacles en masse like schools of fish that never collide. Watch as the light floods through the magnificent clerestory windows captured so dramatically by Hal Morey's famous 1934 photograph. Look at the restored celestial-blue ceiling as it winks with its fiber-optic and gold-leaf constellations. Finally, visit the Campbell Apartment, a truly bizarre cocktail lounge, which from 1923 to 1941 was the private office and salon of New York Central Railroad trustee, John Campbell. He had the room designed to resemble a 13th-century Florentine palazzo with stained-glass windows and an intricately carved, timbered ceiling.

OYSTER VAULT

3 The Grand Central Oyster Bar & Restaurant

141

URBAN GARDEN GEM

4 Paley Park
5 East 53rd Street

An oasis in a concrete jungle, this delightful tiny park dating from 1967 uses its intensely urban setting to its advantage. A massive waterfall obliterates the sound of traffic, and 17 honey-locust trees provide welcome shade for a peaceful lunch. The park was funded by William Paley, former chairman of CBS, who was involved in every aspect of the design, right down to the selection of the hot dog stand. Paley Park was a favorite spot of urban theorist William "Holly" Whyte, who, when the park first opened, used time-lapse photography to show how people used public urban spaces.

ALL THE ART YOU CAN EAT

5 MoMA + The Bar Room at The Modern
11 and 44 West 53rd Street

The Museum of Modern Art has returned from temporary exile in Queens and reopened in its 53rd Street home, newly renovated by Yoshio Taniguchi and expanded to nearly twice the capacity of the former facility. Top off your visit to this mammoth art theme park with refreshments at The Bar Room at The Modern. With views over the Sculpture Garden and a seasonal outdoor terrace, this least formal of the museum's restaurants features the French-American cuisine of chef Gabriel Kreuther. Danish furniture and tableware, along with a huge forest image by German artist Thomas Demand, add detail to the open Bentel & Bentel-designed space.

Completed in 1911, Carrère and Hastings Library, designed to house the collection of bibliophile and real-estate millionaire John Astor, is a masterpiece of Beaux Arts design. If you take a tour, a docent will lead you around a dozen or so of the rooms, including one containing Charles Dickens's writing desk. Alternatively you can wander at your leisure through the rows of researchers in the finely restored Rose Main Reading Room or stand in the Astor Hall lobby, seemingly carved from one giant piece of marble, and contemplate the inherent contradictions of an institution built for public access yet financed by robber barons of the late 19th century. The library also puts on many excellent exhibitions, and lunch can be had within paces of its magnificent steps. The Bryant Park Grill is right behind the library in a park that shows outdoor movie classics in the summer, and Ilo is a gourmet restaurant in the Bryant Park Hotel on East 40th Street.

New York's best-loved and most glorious skyscraper is an Art Déco classic. Even if you've seen it a thousand times before, there are moments when it can still take your breath away. When a glancing sunray lifts your gaze to its Nirosta stainless-steel crown – modeled after a Chrysler radiator grille – or at dusk, when its triangular-shaped windows set in layered scallops begin to emit their white light, Van Alen's optimistic vision of the future holds true. You see the 1930 building in your mind's eye, like all of New York, from afar. An up-close visit, however, with your head tilted back, rewards you with a different perspective. Automobile-themed, handcrafted ornaments such as brickwork cars are at the base of the tower and eagles in place of gargoyles lean out at the building's 61st floor. The lofty crown jewel of the building – the Cloud Room, a 1930s speak-easy with pink marble bathrooms and a gleaming bar of Bavarian wood – is out of bounds, unless you have the gall of tour operator Timothy "Speed" Levitch in the documentary *The Cruise*. Until it is restored you will have to content yourself with the lobby, lined with red African marble, the murals and the marquetry on the elevator doors.

In 1947 an international group of architects convened in New York under the supervision of Wallace K. Harrison. Their mission was to produce a home for the newly formed United Nations but, thanks to Le Corbusier's loudly voiced vision, the end result was much more than that. The United Nations complex is nothing short of an architectural icon signaling both modernity and world peace. The optimism of the project was reflected in Hitchcock's lens as he lingeringly drew down the green-tinted glass façade of the Secretariat Building in the opening scene of his 1959 movie *North by Northwest*. Today the interior has a faded quality captured most poignantly by Adam Bartos's photographs in the book *International Territory: The UN 1945–1995*. You can dine with diplomats in the Delegates Dining Room, the windows of which give capacious views across the East River. The term international cuisine is taken very literally at this lunch buffet and every month features a different country's national cuisine.

A suite of wood-paneled rooms is the genteel site for this old-fashioned, no-nonsense tailors' business. The establishment was once patronized by Ernest Hemingway, upon the recommendation of his friend Gerald Murphy – the dapper artist upon whom F. Scott Fitzgerald based the character Dick Driver in *Tender is the Night*. Murphy advised that Steven Salen was a "very good reliable old New York house, no chi-chi." Whether you want an entire wardrobe custom-made for summering on the Riviera or a minor alteration, you can trust a tailor that in 1933 placed an advertisement in *Fortune* magazine reading, "As formal clothes are conspicuous whatever the occasion, it is essential that such clothes be cut only by those who understand the basic laws of dress, otherwise the individual is in grave danger of paying a goodly sum for an entirely unsuitable outfit."

You can't approach the door of Tiffany's without picturing Holly Golightly in Givenchy, dark glasses and pearls, sipping coffee and gazing wistfully at the treasures displayed in the window. If, like Holly in *Breakfast at Tiffany's*, your "reds" can be soothed away by a small, pale-blue box, then head for this emporium of expensive jewels. Established in 1837, the store enjoyed its heyday at the turn of the 20th century, when Louis Comfort Tiffany, son of the store's founder, began designing his famous lamps and decadent Art Nouveau jewelry and enamels. Today the store's star designers are Elsa Peretti and Paloma Picasso.

Urban Center Books is a bookstore piled high, on the central table and the floor, with literature on urban affairs, architecture and the allied arts. It holds regular architecture-related talks, events and exhibits.

When the original Brasserie, located in the basement of Mies van der Rohe's Seagram building, was destroyed by fire, architects Diller + Scofidio redesigned the restaurant with a nod to its heritage. As patrons had to descend perilously steep steps in the past, a new central glass staircase was introduced, pitched at a shallow angle. Interior details include flat-screen video monitors above the bar capturing diners' abrupt entry from the reception area, tables that are slabs of translucent lime-cast resin, and white leather "Executives" chairs by Eero Saarinen. Chef Luc Dimnet has created a contemporary menu with Brasserie classics indicated in bold face. For dessert, the Moorish chocolate beignets are perfect for sharing.

Since 1985 Linda Dresner has offered clean-lined haute couture at her Park Avenue boutique, and is credited with being the first to bring Jil Sander's minimalist garments to New York. Using light as an integral component of the architecture, designer Michael Gabellini employed natural materials such as limestone, marble, granite, black macassar ebony and nickel silver to create an eminently luxurious environment for equally high-caliber couture.

You need to stand on the south side of 57th Street to fully appreciate the Louis Vuitton–Moët Hennessy Tower as it twists and folds its way up 23 stories. Architect Christian de Portzamparc's design proves that, contrary to popular belief, New York's stringent zoning laws do not inhibit experimentation. Portzamparc describes his tower, with its transparent faceted skin, as an homage to the city of glass. A Christian Dior store takes up the building's first two levels, and the administrative offices of Louis Vuitton and its affiliates are on floors 3 to 22. Topping the tower is a spectacular glass cube where a 30-foot-high (9-meter) penthouse is the scene of lavish fashion shows.

Peter Marino designed the interior of this newly opened 20,000-square-foot retail cathedral, in which vintage LV trunks and red hatboxes hang from the ceiling. The interior fittings and furnishings knowingly play upon the Louis Vuitton checkerboard theme, and the largest square is a three-floor high LED screen visible from the street.

This tiny showroom designed by Frank Lloyd Wright in 1954 can hold only five cars, positioned around a circular, sloping ramp – a mini forerunner of the rotunda at the Guggenheim Museum, some 30 blocks up the street. The geometry of the large circular mirror in the ceiling exploits the three-pointed star of Mercedes-Benz.

21 **Algonquin Hotel**

59 West 44th Street

The hotel lobby is the site of the historic Round Table at which, during the heady 1920s, Dorothy Parker pitted her acerbic wit against fellow literati. The Oak Room puts on cabaret acts every night of the week (except Monday), but it is the smaller, round tables of the utterly unfashionable and slightly dusty Blue Bar that you should head for. Its walls are decorated with the artwork of long-time Algonquin regular Al Hirschfeld, and its uniformed waiters with their inscrutable demeanors serve pub fare and well-made Martinis. Just remember Parker's wisdom on that subject: "I like to have a Martini/Two at the very most/After three I'm under the table/After four I'm under the host."

22 **Takashimaya**

693 Fifth Avenue

From lacquered soup bowls to green seaweed flakes to monochromatic flower arrangements, this Japanese department store provides seven floors of accoutrements for recreating a perfectly imperfect wabi-sabi lifestyle. The initial design for the store followed Japanese tradition, which designates the first two floors as gallery space. The 1997 renovation, however, called for 3,000 square feet of this space to be given over to luggage and travel accessories. Design firm S. Russell Groves solved the problem by creating an open grid system of ebonized ash shelves and low tables to display the larger luggage, and vitrines lined with Hunan silk for smaller articles. The top floor is devoted to high-end hair and beauty products, and the basement reveals the restful Tea Box café where you are reminded why it is you are here and not at Macy's.

SOCIAL CLUB

23 Russian Samovar

256 West 52nd Street

Join Russian intellectuals, writers, artists and sometimes
Mikhail Baryshnikov (who is part-owner and frequent
patron) at the long smoky bar for a warming shot of
horseradish vodka. Rousing traditional Russian folk tunes
that are often sung around the piano may persuade you to
stay. Pick from a rainbow of vodkas flavored in-house or
from a menu strong on blinis and caviar, borscht, satsivi
chicken, beef stroganoff and smoked fish. If you don't
have the time to visit the rowdy Russian enclave in
Brooklyn's Brighton Beach, the Russian Samovar is a fine
alternative. Many of the diners and drinkers engage in
gesticulatory repartee with the owner, Roman Kaplan.
One former regular was the poet Joseph Brodsky, and
poetry readings held in his honor regularly take place at
the restaurant.

SPATIAL CRAFTS

24 American Folk Art Museum

45 West 53rd Street

Tod Williams's and Billie Tsien's beautifully considered new
home for the American Folk Art Museum on West 53rd
Street ups the ante for the 2005 opening of Yoshio
Taniguchi's expanded Museum of Modern Art on the same
block. The architects' solution for the interior combines
monumentality and intimacy in perfect proportion. The
museum has opened to much critical acclaim: architectural
commentator Paul Goldberger has likened it to Sir John
Soane's Museum in London for its "truly original spatial
exercises within the townhouse volume." The museum's
exhibitions live up to their surroundings – a recent
breakthrough show was a retrospective of self-taught
outsider artist Henry Darger. The range of decorative,
functional and ceremonial folk art to be found on display
includes pottery, trade signs, quilts and wind-up toys.

25 Times Square

42nd Street and Broadway

New York's most famous square is in fact an elongated intersection where Broadway crosses Fifth Avenue, and was named after the officeblock which housed *The New York Times* in the early 1900s. The newspaper's building was the world's first in 1928 to display a zipper sign, on which the paper posted election returns. Ever since, the buildings around the square have competed for ownership of the biggest and brightest signs. Little Lulu and her Kleenex box, the puffing Camel smoker and the various neon displays that once wowed the passing public now seem quaint exercises in restraint since the recent profusion of kinetic video monitors and jumbo digital displays that have enough candlepower to be visible at noon. Also of note in the Square is the US Armed Forces Recruiting Station, designed by Architecture Research Office.

ROOM WITH A VIEW

26 Rainbow Grill

30 Rockefeller Plaza

When Rockefeller Center was built in 1934, its superlative flourish was the Rainbow Room on the 65th floor of the tallest and most prominent building in the complex. Its chandeliered circular ballroom has seen three-quarters of a century of dance moves played out across its floor. Today the Rainbow Room is available for private events only, and so you must content yourself with a drink or an expensive meal at the Rainbow Grill. Arrive an hour before sundown to ensure seeing the Empire State Building and all the buildings of southern Manhattan bathed in an orange glow. The men get the added bonus of a great view to the north across Central Park from the window of their restroom.

PAPER ART

27 Kinokuniya

10 West 49th Street

This Manhattan branch of global brand Kinokuniya is a bit of a mess, but that just makes locating your manga, graphic novels, origami paper, and exquisite Japanese stationery and notebooks all the more rewarding.

SENSURBOUND CINEMA

28 Ziegfeld Theater

141 West 54th Street

This fabulous movie theater sits on the site of the original "Ziegfeld Follies." Its massive screen, elegant red décor and impeccable sound and projection quality make it the perfect venue for the kinds of big-action epics where you want to share your gasps and tears with 1,200 others.

PIANO FORTE

29 Steinway & Sons

109 West 57th Street

Steinway & Sons was founded in 1853 by German immigrant Henry Engelhard Steinway in a loft on Varick Street. The first piano produced by the company, number 483, was sold to a New York family for $500 and is now displayed at the Metropolitan Museum of Art. In response to huge demand – thanks to the piano's role as the Victorian answer to a TV – the Steinway business grew to include a factory town in Astoria, Queens, and a 2,000-seat concert hall on 14th Street. The remaining bastion of the piano-maker's empire is a neoclassical showroom on 57th Street designed in the mid-1920s by Grand Central Station's architects, Warren and Wetmore. Behind the two-story rotunda you will find a stunning display, several soundproofed rooms deep, of every kind of grand, baby grand and upright in every finish imaginable.

QUIETLY ECLECTIC

30 City Club Hotel

120

INTIMATE TERMS

31 Single Room Occupancy

158

PORTABLE GLASS AND STEEL

32 Mies + Design Shop

319 West 47th Street

Chris Masaoay, former buyer for the Cooper-Hewitt's museum shop, stocks this Hell's Kitchen design outpost with housewares, gadgets and collectibles that reflect the aesthetic spirit of its modernist namesake.

Upper East Side
Upper West Side
Harlem

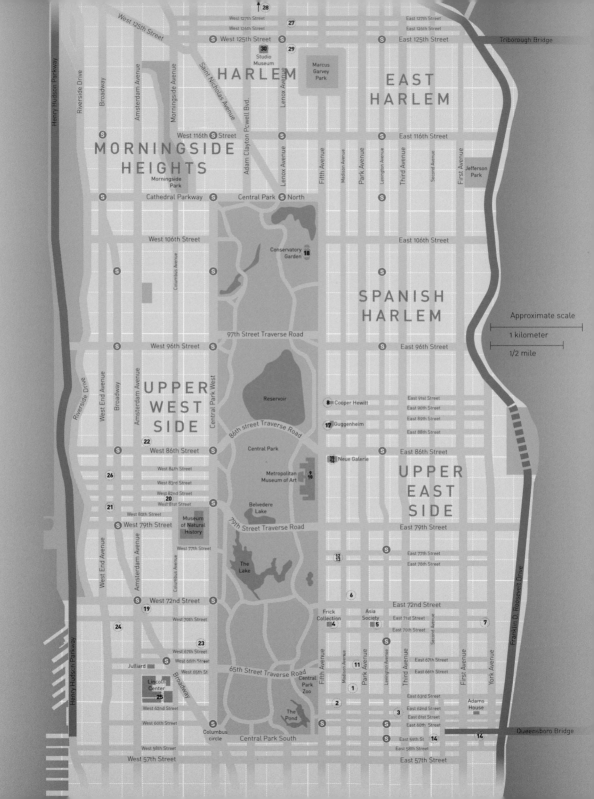

28

West 127th Street
West 126th Street
27

West 125th Street ⓢ   ⓢ East 125th Street

East 126th Street
East 125th Street   Triborough Bridge

30 Studio Museum   **29**

HARLEM   Marcus Garvey Park

EAST HARLEM

West 116th Street ⓢ Street   ⓢ   ⓢ East 116th Street

MORNINGSIDE HEIGHTS

Morningside Park

Jefferson Park

Cathedral Parkway ⓢ   ⓢ Central Park ⓢ North

East 106th Street

Conservatory Garden **18**

SPANISH HARLEM

West 96th Street ⓢ   ⓢ East 96th Street

UPPER WEST SIDE

Reservoir

8 Cooper Hewitt   East 91st Street
East 90th Street
17 Guggenheim   East 89th Street
East 88th Street

West 86th Street   Central Park   **15** Neue Galerie   East 86th Street

22

26   West 84th Street
West 83rd Street
West 82nd Street   Metropolitan Museum of Art   **9 10**   UPPER EAST SIDE
20 West 81st Street
21   Belvedere Lake
West 80th Street
ⓢ West 79th Street   Museum of Natural History   79th Street Traverse Road   East 79th Street
West 77th Street
East 77th Street
12 13   East 76th Street
The Lake
6

West 72nd Street ⓢ   ⓢ   East 72nd Street
19   West 70th Street
24   Frick Collection **4**   Asia Society **5**   East 71st Street
East 70th Street   **7**
West 67th Street
23   West 66th Street ⓢ
Julliard   West 65th St   65th Street Traverse Road   ⓢ   East 67th Street
East 66th Street
Lincoln Center
25   West 62nd Street   Central Park Zoo   **11**   East 63rd Street
West 60th Street   **1**   Adams House
ⓢ Columbus circle   **2**   East 62nd Street
3   East 61st Street
East 60th Street
Central Park South   ⓢ   ⓢ East 59th St   **14**   **14** Queensboro Bridge
East 58th Street
West 57th Street   East 57th Street

Approximate scale
1 kilometer
1/2 mile

Henry Hudson Parkway
Riverside Drive
Broadway
Amsterdam Avenue
Morningside Avenue
Saint Nicholas Avenue
Adam Clayton Powell Blvd.
Lenox Avenue
Fifth Avenue
Madison Avenue
Park Avenue
Lexington Avenue
Third Avenue
Second Avenue
First Avenue

Riverside Drive
West End Avenue
Amsterdam Avenue
Broadway
Columbus Avenue
Central Park West

Henry Hudson Parkway
West End Avenue
Amsterdam Avenue
Columbus Avenue

Franklin D. Roosevelt Drive
York Avenue

The Upper East Side is one of the city's most enduring prestigious neighborhoods. Its zip code, 10021, is the wealthiest in the nation and explains the concentration of classy boutiques and European patisseries on Madison Avenue. The original owners of the Fifth and Park Avenue mansions, families such as the Whitneys, the Astors, the Straights, the Dillons, the Dukes, the Mellons and the Pulitzers, all moved here from downtown in the late 1800s once Central Park was opened. Today many of these grand homes house the city's most venerable museums.

The Upper West Side has its own museums such as the American Museum of Natural History with its newly added Rose Center for Earth and Space, an enormous white sphere suspended in a glass and wire cube. Its residents are stereotypically thought of as intellectually and politically liberal. The UWS is also known for its grand apartment buildings such as the Art Déco–style San Remo, with its ornate twin towers concealing water tanks, and the Dakota on the west edge of the park at 72nd Street, which is, at 120 years old, a grandfather of a New York luxury apartment. The Dakota (named as a joke at the time of its building in 1884 for its "far western" location) is a sought-after address, despite its notoriety as the location for the disturbing movie *Rosemary's Baby* and the place where resident John Lennon was shot. Strawberry Fields, Yoko Ono's memorial to the Beatle, landscaped by Bruce Kelly in 1983, is just a little way into the park outside the Dakota.

The area of Manhattan north of Central Park was covered with wooded hills and valleys and inhabited by Indians when the Dutch started the settlement of Nieuw Haarlem in 1658. A late-19th-century building boom, stimulated by the extension of subways to the north of the island, went bust and African–Americans who had been pushed out of other areas began to rent the empty apartment buildings. By the 1910s Harlem had become the biggest black community in the United States and all through the 1920s and 1930s blacks streamed in from the southern states to feed a black cultural explosion known as the Harlem Renaissance. The Sugar Cane Club and Cotton Club hosted Count Basie, Duke Ellington, and countless others. Lena Horne got her start here, and literary giants Langston Hughes and James Baldwin were native sons. Today, although Harlem's historic liberators and orators are written into its streets and institutions and even though a handful of jazz clubs still survive, the neighborhood is mostly forward-looking. Violent crime, which had plagued its streets, has been significantly reduced and in 2001 former President Bill Clinton moved his office to 55 West 125th Street, just two factors in a widespread revitalization that makes Harlem the neighborhood to watch.

Matthew Kenney's newest restaurant takes his "C" theme to new uptown heights. The previous two downtown sisters are Canteen and Commune. Commissary has a sleek setting created by David Schefer Design using wraparound windows, black-stained floors and a polished white circular bar for dramatic emphasis. Pistachio-and-anise-crusted halibut, roasted cod glazed with vinegar and Riesling and tender venison chops paired with a juniper-and-celery-root gratin are just some of the Italian and Asian-influenced dishes on Kenney's modern American menu. The bar area beneath the custom-designed chandelier is a great place to join flirty-somethings for an after-shopping martini.

This lavish mansion, the former home of the steel and railway tycoon Henry Clay Frick, houses a remarkable collection of paintings by all the weighty European masters. The intimate size of the museum, set back from Fifth Avenue by an elevated garden and a tranquil interior court planted with exotic palms, orchids and ferns and centered on an enormous fountain, make the Frick one of New York's most manageable and memorable museum experiences. Holbein's *Sir Thomas More*, Bellini's *St. Francis in the Desert* and Ingres's *The Comtesse d'Hausonville* are just some of the treasures to behold in its four sumptuous rooms. Take a moment to look through the cast-iron gate from East 70th Street at the garden designed in 1977 by Russell Page. And, if you have time, wander up the leafy block towards the Asia Society for a tasting menu of architectural styles. The elegant houses that line this street range from an 1863 white-painted brownstone at no. 129 to an International Style edifice at no. 124, designed in 1940 by William Lescaze.

Bartholomew Voorsanger is the architect of the recently reconfigured Asia Society on the corner of a leafy block of East 70th Street. He opened up the building's lobby and enclosed it partially in glass, then connected the building's four public floors with a free-floating staircase with white steel supports, blue laminated glass steps and light birch rails. The permanent gallery displays Korean ceramics, Indian miniatures, Japanese Buddhist paintings, Indonesian textiles and Thai sculptures and the temporary exhibitions focus on various themes in pan-Asian culture. Be sure to stop awhile in the skylit Garden Court Café.

The Rhinelander mansion building in which the Lauren fantasy world of WASPy privilege unfolds was originally designed in the 1890s by Kimball & Thompson. The 1980s renovation saved antique fixtures and original mouldings. To amplify the aura of a leisure-filled lifestyle of a fictionalized prewar English gentility, the decorators added antique display furniture, Persian carpets, vintage riding boots, Vuitton trunks, cashmere upholstery, camelhair drapes, antique Baccarat chandeliers and Lalique panels.

On the ground floor of the Richard Gluckman–designed New York headquarters of Sotheby's is a restaurant for dealers and collectors who've worked up an appetite on the auction floor. Dineen Nealy Architects have created a space that they describe as "clubby." Its laurel-wood walls showcase a revolving selection of art in a less formal context than that provided by the offices and galleries on the upper floors. The restaurant exudes an atmosphere of comfort, thanks in part to the muted color scheme and the use of soft materials, such as calfskin and chenille upholstery. The culinary emphasis is on contemporary American seasonal fare, and the prix-fixe menu might include braised lobster with corn relish, sautéed quail with bacon and salsify and grey sole with Manila clams and summer truffles.

8 Cooper–Hewitt National Design Museum
2 East 91st Street

Cooper–Hewitt National Design Museum sits under the imperial umbrella of the Smithsonian Institution and is the only museum in the United States devoted exclusively to historic and contemporary design. Its collections of 250,000 objects and exhibitions – such as "National Design Triennial: Inside Design Now" – are housed in the former home of industrial magnate Andrew Carnegie. The 64-room mansion, built from 1899 to 1902, is a challenging environment in which to present modern design, but its curators keep trying. The Arthur Ross Terrace and Garden, which is the scene of DJ sessions and many design-related gatherings in the summer, is a bucolic bonus to your visit.

THE MOTHER OF ALL MUSEUMS
9 The Metropolitan Museum of Art
1000 Fifth Avenue

It's beyond huge. It's overwhelming. Even the long-distance runners among art lovers will need to take care to pace themselves in this venerable museum. Many of the Met's departments are extensive enough to be museums in themselves and it is advisable to treat them as such, one day at a time. The American Wing holds one of the most comprehensive collections of American painting and sculpture in the world. In the decorative arts section, seek out the Frank Lloyd Wright living room.

SANDWICHES AND SCULPTURE IN A ROOFSCAPE
10 Iris and B. Gerald Cantor Roof Garden
Metropolitan Museum of Art, 1000 Fifth Avenue

If you do nothing else, and providing it is some time between the month of May and late fall, you should ascend to the Iris and B. Gerald Cantor Roof Garden where, every year, a new sculpture show is installed. You can enjoy a sandwich and a drink and look over the treetops of Central Park as the sun dips behind them. A glorious finale to a day of art appreciation.

TIFFANY CENTERPIECE
11 Seventh Regiment Armory
640 Park Avenue

The venue for numerous art and antique fairs, this fantastic French medieval-style fortress is a treasure in itself. The Tiffany Room, encrusted with decorative stained glass, mosaic and metalwork, is the only existing example of Louis Comfort Tiffany's lavish interior design in the city. Upstairs is the Seventh Regiment Mess and Lounge, a faded 1950s time capsule of a restaurant.

MAGNET FOR BIBLIOPHILES
12 Ursus Rare Books
Carlyle Hotel, 981 Madison Avenue

A comprehensive selection of art reference books, superb copies of rare books in all fields and antique decorative prints can be found and browsed in this well-established store on the mezzanine of the Carlyle Hotel. Peter Kraus's collection is particularly strong in the areas of art, architecture, literature, travel and illustrated children's books. You might find a copy of *Alice in Wonderland* signed by Alice Liddell or a first edition of Ludwig Bemelmans's *Madeline* to put you in the mood for the author and artist's namesake bar downstairs.

CHILDHOOD MEMORIES IN A PIANO BAR
13 Bemelmans Bar
Carlyle Hotel, 35 East 76th Street

The walls of this dimly lit piano bar were painted by Ludwig Bemelmans, a 1940s Carlyle resident. The characters from his famous *Madeline* books are depicted in seasonal Central Park settings and their whimsical charm provides a soothing backdrop for various sequestered celebrities and their afternoon cocktails.

HEAD FOR THE HEIGHTS
14 The Roosevelt Island Tramway
59th Street and Second Avenue
Guastavino's
409 East 59th Street

For one of the most spectacular views of New York – and at the mere price of a subway token – take a return trip on the Roosevelt Island Tramway. Built by the Swiss company Vonroll under designers Prentice & Chan and Ohlhausen, the aerial tramway has been used since 1976 to shuttle Roosevelt Island residents to and from Manhattan. During the four-minute ride, you are quietly whisked 250 feet (75 meters) above the East River, from where you can gaze up and down the water and along the high-rise canyons of Midtown. On your return you'll find sustenance in the monumental vaulted space beneath the Queensboro Bridge. Guastavino, British design guru Terence Conran's stylish restaurant, was created in collaboration with Hardy Holzman Pfeiffer Associates, who meticulously restored the ribbed-tile vaulting by Rafael Guastavino y Esposito.

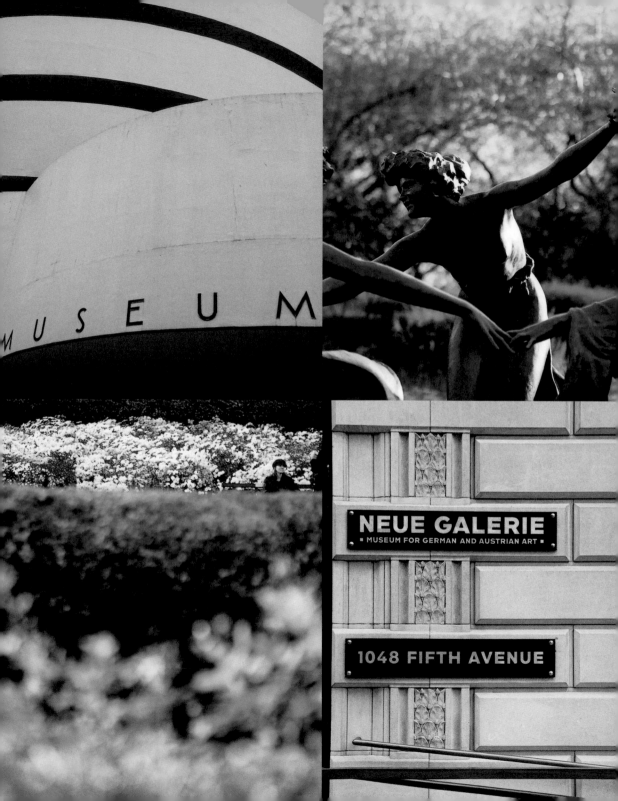

15 Neue Galerie

1048 Fifth Avenue

The collection of this small museum is dedicated to early-20th-century German and Austrian art. The original landmark building is a very fine mansion, dating from 1914, but it is the exquisitely restrained interior restoration at the hands of Annabelle Selldorf that will bring your applause. The paintings, sculptures and art objects stand out dramatically against Selldorf's quiet yet luminous environments. She has also isolated the major architectural features of the building, designed by Carrère and Hastings, so the spiraling marble and wrought-iron stair, the domed skylight and the marble and wood wainscoting can be appreciated.

16 Café Sabarsky

Neue Galerie, 1048 Fifth Avenue

Café Sabarsky is the museum's excellent eatery, operated by Kurt Gutenbrunner, chef and owner of the acclaimed restaurant Wallsé. With its black-and-white tiled floor, lighting fixtures by Josef Hoffman, furniture by Adolf Loos and banquettes upholstered in an Otto Wagner fabric, Sabarsky draws inspiration from the Viennese cafés that were the centers of intellectual and artistic activity in the early 20th century. The menu focuses on traditional Austrian dishes and does not omit specialties such as strudel and Linzertorte.

17 Solomon R. Guggenheim Museum

1071 Fifth Avenue

Set amid the restrained and opulent apartment buildings that line Central Park's eastern side, Frank Lloyd Wright's fantastic white spiraling edifice edges into view as you walk up Fifth Avenue. Opened in 1959 to considerable excitement and controversy, the museum represents the highpoint of America's best-known modern architect. And if the building itself weren't enough reason to visit, the collection is outstanding. Coiling your way down from the top, you will encounter Peggy Guggenheim's trove of Cubist, Surrealist and Abstract Expressionist works and the outstanding photography collection that holds more than 200 Robert Mapplethorpes. You will end up in the atrium below, where an impressive Friday-night music program, often tied to the current exhibition, takes place.

18 Conservatory Gardens, Central Park

Fifth Avenue and 105th Street

Central Park divides the two "Uppers," which tend to feel like estranged sisters. The people who live in these neighborhoods are fiercely loyal to their locale, so it is not uncommon to find people who have not gone to the "other side" for decades. The park itself is a design masterpiece. "Every foot of the park's surface, every tree and bush, as well as every arch, roadway and walk, has been placed where it is with a purpose," said its landscape architect, Frederick Law Olmsted. When, in 1857, the park began to be transformed from a dump and a bone-boiling plant into an urban idyll, it was surrounded only by open country and squatter shacks. The park's fringes were quickly developed, the biggest surge taking place between 1900 and 1920. Most of these buildings exhibit neo-Georgian, neo-Federal, neo-French or neo-Italian Renaissance styling. Aid your cultural digestion with a stroll through the symmetrical walks of the three formal gardens that constitute the Conservatory Gardens. These gardens – English, Italian and French – were added to Central Park's evolving grand plan in the 1930s, replacing the mouldering greenhouses established by the park's first gardener, Ignaz Pilat. Six acres (2.5 hectares) of hedges, canopied crab-apple trees, beautifully manicured lawns, a trellis of wisteria, profusions of flowers, fountains and more await you in this seldom-visited corner of the park.

19 72nd Street Subway

72nd Street and Broadway

Make your entrance to the Upper West Side via this Flemish Renaissance–style subway station control house, which occupies its own island at 72nd Street and Broadway. Designed in 1904 by Heins & Lafarge, it has just been restored using the same materials as the original.

20 Maxilla and Mandible

451 Columbus Avenue

Just one block north of the American Museum of Natural History is a showroom where you can actually take the natural history exhibits home. Specimens from around the world, including bones and skeletons, fossils, eggs, insects, seashells and the supplies necessary to their display can be found in this emporium of anatomical, paleontological, osteological and entomological oddities.

Even though you'll want to stop still and gaze around at the crazy interior of this New York institution, you'll be moved on by the sharp elbows of primarily Jewish shoppers focused intently on their purchases of hand-sliced nova, rye bread, challah and chicken pot pie. The smells of cheese, fresh bagels and ground coffee pull you up and down the aisles, on the shelves of which imported packages of dried fruits and biscuits teeter perilously. This food bazaar gives you a real taste of New York.

For a perfect drink before a performance at Lincoln Center, make your way to the hidden wood-paneled bar at the back of this romantic old-world restaurant. The neo-Gothic Hotel des Artistes was designed in 1917 by George Mort Pollard. The studio apartments did not have kitchens but its tenants, although they were all artists, were hardly of the starving variety. They could congregate in the café, wrapped with Howard Chandler Christy's mural of frolicking nude nymphs, for bistro food and conversation or send fresh ingredients to the kitchens via dumbwaiters and receive meals in return. Among the hotel's most famous residents were Isadora Duncan, Noel Coward, Rudolf Valentino and Norman Rockwell.

24 Café Luxembourg
200 West 70th Street

The 1980s take on an Art Déco interior includes a zinc bar, wicker chairs, black-and-white terrazzo floor and dairy wall tiles. The eclectic bistro menu is perfect for pre-opera grazing. Sit at the bar for some fried oysters and Champagne, elbow to elbow with discerning celebrities who weren't up for the trek 90 blocks south to the Odeon.

CULTURAL MEGAPLEX
25 Lincoln Center for the Performing Arts
65th Street at Columbus Avenue

Even if you do not have tickets to see Plácido Domingo in *Andrea Chénier*, it is worth standing for a few moments at the center of this vast performing arts complex to soak up the urban scene. Bejeweled music- and ballet-lovers criss-cross the plaza or wait for their dates on the edge of the central fountain. A variety of performance spaces were built in the late 1950s and 1960s by the stars of the day, such as Philip Johnson (state theater), Eero Saarinen (repertory theater) and Max Abramovitz (philharmonic hall). The Metropolitan Opera House, designed by Wallace K. Harrison in 1966 and featuring enormous Marc Chagall paintings, is a spectacular venue in which to see a Met production under the artistic direction of James Levine.

UPMARKET AMERICAN BRASSERIE
26 Ouest
2315 Broadway

This New American brasserie uses tall padded circular booths to create intimate cocoons in a dining place of dramatic scale. Chef-owner Tom Valenti's acclaimed menu offers such dishes as house-smoked sturgeon with frisée, lardons and a poached egg that reference the smoked-fish-and-bagels neighborhood's heritage. For the entrées, however, it leans on bold preparations of meat and poultry.

FOOD FOR THE SOUL

27 Sylvia's Soul Food Restaurant

328 Lenox Avenue (Malcolm X Boulevard)

For hot ribs, coconut cake and some Southern comfort, pop into Sylvia's joint. Sylvia and Herbert Woods met in a South Carolina bean field when they were 11 and 12 years old, respectively. They married in 1943 and set up their soul food restaurant in 1962. The restaurant has expanded from an original capacity of 35 to fill almost an entire block, but it remains a wholly African–America-owned and -run business. Try the gospel lunch after Sunday services at the Abyssinian Baptist Church.

GOSPEL CHURCH

28 Abyssinian Baptist Church

132 Odell Clark Place

Built in 1923 by Charles W. Bolton, this blue-stone neo-Gothic church is renowned for its late pastor, Adam Clayton Powell, Jr., the first black congressman from New York City. Services are at 9:00 a.m. and 11:00 a.m. on Sundays.

HARLEM JAZZ DEN

29 Lenox Lounge

288 Lenox Avenue (Malcolm X Boulevard)

This legendary lounge, specifically the Zebra room, has played host to Billie Holiday, Miles Davis and John Coltrane, among others. The original Art Déco interior with zebra-striped walls, tiled floor and padded leather ceiling has been restored, but the history of Harlem's premier jazz venue (now that the Cotton Club and the Savoy Ballroom have gone) still hangs in the air like smoke.

AFRICAN–AMERICAN ARTS

30 The Studio Museum in Harlem

144 West 125th Street (Dr. Martin Luther King, Jr. Boulevard)

The museum's unique focus on African–American art and that of the African Diaspora has produced some groundbreaking exhibitions under the curatorial guidance of exhibition director, Thelma Golden. Central to the museum's mission is the challenging of canonical histories of European and American Modernism. The vibrant artists-in-residence program produces regular showings of emerging artists who work in the studio areas of the building. For lunch at Sylvia's you need only cross the street.

Williamsburg
Long Island City
DUMBO

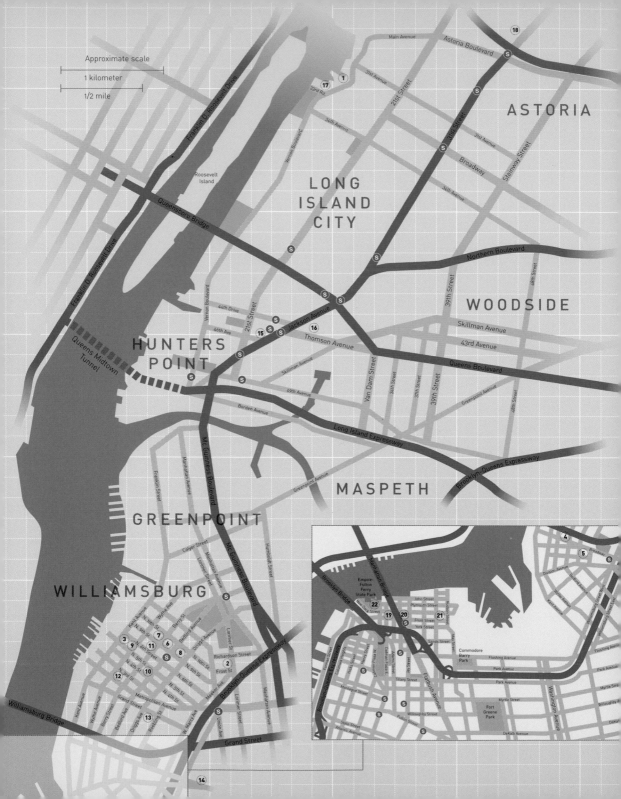

With what to locals seems like improbable velocity, the Brooklyn neighborhood of Williamsburg has in a few short years transformed itself from a declining industrial district to an artists' enclave and hipster destination spot. In the mid-1800s Williamsburg was a fashionable resort area, with hotels, clubs and beer gardens clustered around the Brooklyn ferry park attracting industrialists and professionals. Once the Williamsburg Bridge was opened, the neighborhood became increasingly industrialized. Williamsburg native Henry Miller remembered "the ironworks where the red furnace glowed and men walked toward the glowing pit with huge shovels in their hands" of the 1890s. At that time the waterfront was cluttered with docks, shipyards, warehouses, taverns, mills and breweries. Today there are fewer than 9,000 manufacturing jobs (compared to 93,000 in 1961). Fortunately, there is still enough of an eclectic ethnic mix of Puerto Ricans, Poles and Hasidim to prevent the burgeoning scene from becoming too homogeneous. Thanks to the idiosyncratic shops and relaxed attitude, on weekday afternoons the area has a quiet, almost villagelike, atmosphere. But already many of the artists who forged the way in the early 1990s for the flood of galleries have been priced out of the lofts they once squatted.

As yet there is no hotel in the neighborhood, so stay in Manhattan and take the L train three stops from Union Square. Bedford Avenue, the main drag, and the streets between North 9th and Broadway that cross it, are dotted with enough boutiques, antique shops, galleries, cafés, restaurants and bars to keep you happily occupied for an afternoon that may well turn into night.

Long Island City, several miles to the north of Williamsburg, is another wind-swept industrial zone, with some residential pockets of Asian and Latin American immigrants, that is undergoing revitalization thanks to a growing art, film and design community. New York seems to have fixed its greedy gaze on Long Island City in the sprawling borough of Queens that has, until now, remained a frontier to most Manhattanites. The advanced guard has already installed itself in choice lofts, and it may not be long before Long Island City, just like Williamsburg, has its corner bodegas turned into cappuccino-serving cafés playing electronica.

The 19th-century brick warehouses of the area between the Manhattan and Brooklyn Bridges, known as DUMBO, are dense with the workshops and studios of artists and designers. With real estate development in full swing, a Starbucks already in place and a growing contingent of home furnishings boutiques and cafés, it looks as if the artists will soon be going the way of the longshoremen who previously populated the area.

Set on the Long Island City bank of the East River with Midtown high-rises as a backdrop, this outdoor sculpture park is the site of large-scale works by both emerging and recognized artists. Socrates Sculpture Park was an abandoned riverside landfill and illegal dumpsite until 1986, when a coalition of artists and community members, under the leadership of artist Mark di Suvero, transformed it into both an open studio and exhibition space and a neighborhood park for local residents. Exhibitions rotate on a semi-annual basis; a visit to Socrates a month or two preceding an opening allows a glimpse into the sculpture-making process.

You will discover the real charm of this old-fashioned bar in a 1900s brick storefront in the narrow, curtained-off back room, which features an upholstered vaudeville stage lit with vanity bulbs. This room, padded like the interior of a jewel box, hosts nightly performances by local bluegrass bands and poets, booked by co-owner Juliana Nash. Bingo and trivia quiz nights on Tuesdays and Wednesdays are wildly popular with the vintage T-shirt-and-trucker's-cap set.

MOROCCAN-MOSAIC RESTAURANT

6 Oznot's Dish

79 Berry Street

There are two times of the day when this Moroccan-infused restaurant shines brightest. One is the brunching hour that stretches between noon and 3 p.m., and involves such unusual takes on breakfast fare as cardamom French toast with raisins, nutmeg, yogurt and fresh fruit, and poached eggs wrapped in cured salmon on corn frittatas. You'll sit with families and gallery-goers on mismatched chairs in the main room or in the sunny, greenhouse-like lean-to at the back of the restaurant. The other is at twilight, when you can perch at the mosaic-encrusted bar and sample from the extensive wine list.

EMERGING TENDENCIES

7 Momenta Art

72 Berry Street

Momenta Art is a not-for-profit exhibition space directed by artist Eric Heist. Its two-person shows, with a bias toward American artists, and its thematic exhibits such as "Pop Patriotism," curated in response to the national surge of flagwaving after 9/11, are consistently thought-provoking. For each exhibition in this pristine white box of a space, the gallery publishes a newsletter that includes information about the artists and their works.

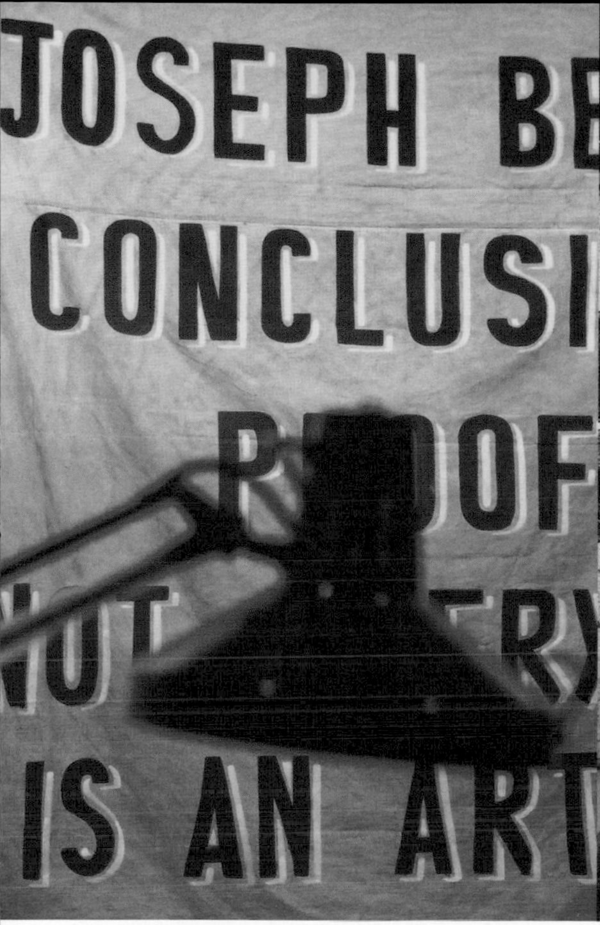

8 Pierogi 2000

177 North 9th Street

The name of this gallery, one of the most established in the neighborhood, is a reference to the dumpling favored by the vicinity's Polish residents. Pierogi 2000 has monthly shows featuring the work of artists from Williamsburg, Brooklyn, and beyond. You can riffle through samples of work from more than 500 mostly American artists, as long as you don the white gloves provided. The original unframed works stored in flat files are affordable and include the work of such notables as Lawrence Weiner, Keith Tyson and Bob and Roberta Smith.

WILLIAMSBURG'S ART BAR

9 Galapagos

70 North 6th Street

You enter this bar and performance space, barely signaled from the street by a red light, via a metal walkway that bridges an oily dark reflecting pool. The converted mayonnaise factory is the venue for Monday evening burlesque shows in the candlelit bar area and a myriad of experimental performances, underground film screenings, album launch parties and book readings in the garage-like back space.

INDEPENDENT BOOKSTORE
10 Spoonbill & Sugartown
218 Bedford Avenue

Located in the Realform Girdle Building smack in the center of Williamsburg's thoroughfare of cool, Spoonbill & Sugartown restores your confidence in the survival of the independent bookstore. Specializing in used, rare and new books on contemporary art, art history, architecture and design, the store numbers among its staff some large sleepy cats that drape themselves over the piles of volumes waiting to be shelved.

OLD FOR NEW
11 The Future Perfect

166

DINER CAR
12 Relish
225 Wythe Avenue

A location scout's fantasy, this silver diner with original fittings and its idyllic patio is one of Williamsburgers' favorite hangouts. The food is comfort-oriented, exemplified by classics such as cheeseburgers and jumbo "tobacco" onion rings coated in cinnamon and cayenne spice batter. The self-consciously cool waiting staff play their own mix CDs and bestow their slight attention on your dining needs when it suits them.

CLUB ROCK
13 TRASH
256 Grand Street

The unofficial headquarters of the Electroclash revolution and the initiator of hedonistic gay night, "Berliniamsburg," this lurid rock club (formerly known as Luxx) owned by Larry Tee has attracted a devoted following of 30-something club kids. Reflective wallpaper and a high-tech sound system add a dose of glamor to the vibe.

BIKERS' BAR
14 Moto
394 Broadway

Motorbike enthusiasts Billy Phelps and John McCormick converted a decrepit check-cashing joint into a motorcycle-themed no-frills bar with a snacking menu. Situated in the Hassidic-Jewish-meets-Puerto Rican community of south Williamsburg, the bar prefigures the imminent southward development of the Williamsburg neighborhood.

15 P.S.1 Contemporary Art Center
22–25 Jackson Avenue

The corridors of the converted Public School No. 1 now echo with the clickety-clack sound of Prada-heeled contemporary art lovers. Be sure to seek out the James Turrell Room at dusk for a sublime encounter with a square-shaped patch of shifting sky. And for non-claustrophobes, find Robert Wogan's fourth-floor installation, a pitch-black passageway that narrows until ejecting you into a pyramid-shaped room showing a video of the pre-renovated P.S.1. Each year the courtyard is transformed into an urban playground by an emerging architect. The installation, usually water-themed, sets the scene for Saturday afternoon DJ Warm Up Sessions.

TROLLEY CARS TO MODERN ART
16 SculptureCenter
44-19 Purves Street

SculptureCenter, which has been around since 1928, today inhabits a former Long Island City trolley repair shop redesigned in 2002 by Maya Lin, the artist responsible for the Vietnam Veterans' Memorial in Washington, D.C. With more than 9,000 square feet of interior and outdoor exhibition space and an innovative curatorial policy, the center provides an important forum for the conceptual, aesthetic and material concerns of contemporary sculpture, as well as staging solo exhibitions of such artists as Petah Coyne and Rita McBride.

SCULPTED TRANQUILITY
17 Isamu Noguchi Garden Museum
9-01 33rd Road

Thirteen indoor and outdoor galleries within a converted factory building encircle a tranquil garden containing Noguchi's granite and basalt sculptures. The factory was the studio and storage facility of the Japanese sculptor and designer of furniture, stage sets and public spaces. On exhibition are more than 240 of Noguchi's works, including stone, metal, wood and clay sculptures, and models for public projects and dance sets. His Akari light sculptures are for sale in the museum store-café, enabling you to take a piece of Zen home with you.

CZECH MATE
18 Bohemian Hall & Beer Garden

157

PAINT BRUSH AND A PANNINI
19 DUMBO General Store
111 Front Street

DUMBO (Down Under the Manhattan Bridge Overpass) is the 1980s acronym used to refer to this once industrial (and now residential) waterfront neighborhood, and General Store is the unofficial canteen of its creative community. The wooden tables in this unpolished space will be filled throughout the day with local artists clutching espressos and panninis, along with the tools of their trade, purchased from the selection of art supplies at the rear of the café.

MAGAZINE IN 3-D
20 Spring
126a Front Street

DUMBO's converted industrial buildings contain warrens of artists' studios and design workshops. Some of the resulting artwork can be viewed and purchased at the innovative gallery Spring, or three-dimensional magazine, as the owners, textile designer Steve Butcher and producer Anna Cosentino, refer to it.

BYGONE-ERA BROWNSTONES
21 Vinegar Hill
Between Hudson and Gold Streets

Cut off from the rest of the world by the Navy Yard on one side and the smokestacks of a power plant on the other, Vinegar Hill is an eight-square-block of row houses and lush dooryards that evoke mid-19th-century Brooklyn. Wander the Belgian-block streets lined with charmingly disheveled brownstones, their storefront windows bearing traces of their former commercial lives.

CHOCOLATE CHARMER
22 Jacques Torres
66 Water Street

One of the true pleasures of visiting DUMBO is going to the charming Jacques Torres chocolate boutique, picking out a selection of delicious chocolates patterned with red and gold motifs, and having them boxed in the immaculate packaging. If it's cold, stay for a cup of hot chocolate so thick you can stand your spoon up in it. Otherwise, take your purchases to Brooklyn Bridge Park (also home to the picturesque 1890 Tobacco Inspection Warehouse) and drink in the unsurpassed views of Manhattan.

Park Slope
Smith Street
Fort Greene

"No! Sleep! Till Brooklyn!"The Beastie Boys' rallying cry may have made sense in 1990 but today Brooklyn has enough going on to keep you up all night. Several of its neighborhoods — DUMBO, Smith Street, Fort Greene and Red Hook among them — are sprouting new scenes that have earned them multiple stars on New York's style map.The fastest-developing destination territories tend, unsurprisingly, to be clustered near the three bridges that connect Brooklyn to Lower Manhattan.

Park Slope is the older hippy sister of the bunch. If it doesn't already, it should be able to lay claim to having the largest number of baby strollers per block of anywhere in the nation. It's impossible to carry your soy-milk decaffeinated cappuccino more than a few Birkenstock-shod feet without bumping into another set of proud young parents, often same-sex.The charming brownstones and mansions of this district were built around Prospect Park's Manhattan-facing aspect in the late 1800s after it opened its gates and the Brooklyn Bridge was completed.

Brooklyn's most happening scene is acted out on a section of Smith Street that has its head in Boerum Hill — a neighborhood of brownstones with prices kept in check by the proximity of projects — and its tail in Italianate Carroll Gardens. Until the late 1990s, when an urban renewal project paved the way for pioneering restaurants such as Patois, this stretch of Smith was a no-go zone. Now the street, lined with trees and wrought-iron street lamps, is peopled by shoppers and diners a few years older and some degrees less fashion-obsessed than those found on its rival, Williamsburg's Bedford Avenue. By day you can browse the vintage and contemporary clothes stores as well as the two furniture stores that double as cafés. In the evening you can dine on bistro fare, at Café LuluC or Bar Tabac, or on more sophisticated cuisine at Grocery. Drinking venues range from nicotine-stained classics, such as The Brooklyn Inn, to the contemporary good looks of BarBelow.

The popular image of Fort Greene is one colored by Spike Lee's famously bittersweet portrayals of the artsy, well-educated African-American district in which he came of age. And while the historic district of Fort Greene — with its luscious late-19th-century brownstones that line the streets to the south and east of Fort Greene Park, named for its pivotal role in the Revolutionary War — is still characterized by the racial and economic diversity that Lee documented, the nightlife around Lafayette and DeKalb Avenues is an utterly contemporary phenomenon. French bistros such as Loulou, Chez Oscar, Ici and Liquors cater for the Brooklyn Academy of Music (BAM) crowds and an ever-increasing local population of young professionals, reaping the benefits of an area rich in black culture.

Known for its annual Cherry Blossom Festival, the Brooklyn Botanic Garden is among the best-regarded in the country. Stroll beneath wisteria-laden trellises to the rose garden boasting 1,200 different varieties. The recently restored Japanese garden features a teahouse overlooking a pond seething with turtles and giant koi. A blue heron, a frequent visitor to the pond, completes the tranquil scene. The greenhouses contain one of the world's largest collections of bonsai trees, some well over 100 years old. Founded in 1910, the Brooklyn Botanic Garden has far more charm than its larger counterpart in the Bronx.

The Brooklyn Museum of Art is the second largest art museum in the city and one of the largest in the US. Although acquiring a certain notoriety following the withdrawl of funding for the 1999 "Sensation" exhibition, the museum boasts a magnificent permanent collection, which includes more than a million objects, ranging from ancient Egypt to contemporary America. The façade of the 19th-century Beaux Arts building has been recently renovated, and has acquired a new entrance pavilion. Music and entertainment programs take place on the first Saturday of each month.

Assembled in this diminutive store are exotically hued textiles, home furnishings, gold chandelier earrings, and clothing handpicked from India, Turkey and Lebanon.

A classic old-time Brooklyn establishment dating from 1868, the inn features a large, ornate antique bar, huge mirrors and a high tin ceiling. During the day, light streams in through the dusty windows falling on the open notebooks and discarded pens of the hard-drinking regulars, who seem to include a disproportionate number of writers. Argue about Kierkegaard or play a neighborly game of pool in the back room. At night, the place can fill up with young professionals back from a hard day in "the city." With only a neon Pilsner Urquell sign on its neo-Gothic iron-and-wood exterior, you'll need to follow the locals to find this corner spot.

Husband-and-wife team Jennifer Argenta and Anthony Nelson offer Brooklyn boys a selection of labels that ranges from such UK style staples as Duffer St George and Ben Sherman, to sporty American favorites like Original Penguin and Fred Perry.

Thirteen simple paper-topped tables in an unadorned storefront constitute this restaurant, which, with its flavorful seasonal American fare, transcends mere neighborhood status. Co-chefs and owners, Charles Kiely and Sharon Pachter, take the time to chat as they bring you your house-made sausage, marinated skirt steak, or duck in caramelized wine sauce. Fresh market produce, meat and fish are the foundation stones of Grocery's cuisine. On summer nights you can sit out back beneath a spreading fig tree in the ivy-walled garden.

WORLD'S BEST CHEESECAKE
12 Junior's
386 Flatbush Avenue

From the day Harry Rosen opened Junior's on Flatbush Avenue in 1950, three generations of his family have been baking "the world's most fabulous cheesecakes" and mixing egg creams for locals and those who venture across the Manhattan Bridge. The flashing lights of its signage are particularly photogenic.

THE SOUL OF JAZZ
13 Frank's Lounge
660 Fulton Street

Any single aspect of this bar, when taken alone, would be uninspired: shabby carpet, low ceiling and dark paneling. But to go to Frank's Lounge on a Thursday, when Lonnie Youngblood is blowing his saxophone and the old-timers are holding court, is to be transported back in time to a Fort Greene that existed before Spike Lee and the Notorious B.I.G., and to feel the soul behind what would become the hip-hop heart of New York.

PERFORMANCES ON THE EDGE
14 Brooklyn Academy of Music
30 Lafayette Avenue

This recently restored 19th-century building, the cultural cornerstone of Fort Greene, stages an eclectic mix of opera, dance and experimental performances by the likes of Lou Reed, Philip Glass and Laurie Anderson. BAM, as it is known, also houses BAM Rose Cinemas, arguably the best movie theater in the city. Apart from the regular seasonal performances, BAM also hosts several festivals, including the feted Next Wave Festival, begun in 1983.

VIENNESE WALTZ
15 Thomas Beisl
25 Lafayette Avenue

Until the BAM restaurant is bestowed a much-needed overhaul, Academy visitors are advised to go across the road to Thomas Beisl for pre-show appetizers or post-show desserts. Celebrated Austrian chef-owner Thomas Ferlesch left Café des Artistes (p. 88) to renovate this location into a bistro. A liver terrine with kumquat-cranberry compote, speck and sausage charcuterie, and an inexpensive cheese plate make excellent snacks, while heartier appetites are satiated with beef cheek goulash and schnitzel.

sleep

Spectacular lobbies, hip bars and top-notch restaurants, meticulously orchestrated for seeing and being seen in, have become de rigueur in New York's hotels, the enduring legacy of a hotel-design revolution that began in the 1980s. Hoteliers, with Ian Schrager at their vanguard, teamed up with celebrity interior designers to create a relentlessly designed experience that extends from the vase in the bathroom to the matchbooks in the bar. Now that the boutique-hotel look has been copied and diluted around the world, the establishments presented here are singled out for their departures from the formulaic or for their uniqueness, eclecticism or excess.

106 Bed and Breakfast on the Park

1 113 Prospect Park West, Brooklyn
Rooms from $155

Prospect Park, Frederick Law Olmsted and Calvert Vaux's 1873 vision of a bucolic idyll, provides 536 acres (217 hectares) of leafy respite for overtaxed Brooklynites. On its west side, beyond the 90-acre (36-hectare) greensward known as Long Meadow, and at the crown of the slope that runs down through the village-like neighborhood of Park Slope, is Prospect Park West. The mansions that still grace this avenue were erected in the late 1880s, shortly after the completion of the Brooklyn Bridge enabled easier access to Manhattan. Number 113, a four-story brownstone built in 1892, is one of Brooklyn's top ten landmarks of Victorian architecture. Refashioned in 1987 into a bed and breakfast, it has nine rooms, some with views all the way to the Statue of Liberty and those at the front overlooking the park. Owner Liana Paolella, an antiques dealer as well as innkeeper, has furnished the brownstone with her wares, ranging from the mid 19th to the early 20th centuries, and including some especially fine oil paintings from her family collection. The original mouldings in the parlor are of intricately carved oak, African mahogany and bird's-eye maple. The suite on the top floor has a double canopy bed swathed in French lace, a large antique bath, a sitting area and a private rooftop garden with views of the city skyline. Breakfast is taken in the Victorian dining room, pooled with colored light from the stained-glass bay windows. A feast consisting of homemade bread, German pancakes, crêpes, quiche Lorraine and homemade jams and jellies is spread on the huge table, set with Irish linen, Royal Crown Derby and Waterford jars. Rest assured that you will be well fed for your exploration of the nearby Brooklyn "villages" of Park Slope, Fort Greene and Boerum Hill.

34 **The Maritime Hotel**

9 88 Ninth Avenue
Rooms from $295

Anchored at the point where Chelsea's art galleries meet the Meatpacking District—the site of a recent explosion of boutiques and chic eateries—The Maritime Hotel is the newest creation of Midas-fingered interior stylists Eric Goode and Sean McPherson. Taking this 1966 building's original use as the headquarters for the National Maritime Union as their cue, Goode and McPherson have constructed a hotel with the feel of an elegant 1940s luxury liner. All 120 rooms face west, with views of the magnificent Hudson River sunsets through their 5-foot-wide porthole windows. The rooms, like ship's cabins, are compact, but luxurious details such as burnished teak paneling, sleek shelving, Japanese fabric wall-coverings and C. O. Bigelow bath amenities prevent any feelings of privation. The four penthouse suites have garden terraces replete with the hotel's most decadent feature: heated outdoor showers. The spaces for eating, drinking and relaxing are equally well considered and hugely dramatic. Nowhere is this more evident than in the cavernous Japanese restaurant Matsuri, with its barrel-vaulted ceiling strung with immense paper lanterns hand-painted by owner Mikio Shinagawa's grandfather. The other restaurant is Italian and split into two by a large terrace garden, planted with magnolia trees and hung with globular lanterns. The bar/café with glazed white-brick walls and vintage Italian posters is less formal than the trattoria dining section with its mahogany Art Déco bar, wood-burning oven, and polished wood ceiling. In their quest to create a new interior for the hotel yet remain true to the spirit of the Albert C. Ledner building, Goode and McPherson spent time studying the architecture of Oscar Niemeyer in Brazil and Le Corbusier in France, as well as looking at boat and train interiors. All of the graphic elements were created by design firm Number Seventeen, and the monogrammed carpet and daily weather icons posted in the elevators are particularly nice touches.

66 **City Club Hotel**

30 55 West 44th Street
Rooms from $275

The opening of the City Club Hotel signaled the beginning of a new era of what shall henceforth be known as post-boutiquism. Jeff Klein, a worldly socialite and first-time hotelier, dubs his refined travelers' haven an "anti-boutique" hotel, with an "anti-lobby" to match. Indeed, in contrast to the wonderland that welcomes guests into the Royalton across the road, this lobby is intentionally small and mousy. With its red coffee table piled high with books and vases of orchids, waxed cork flooring and pillow-strewn window-seat, it feels more like the entrance to a private residence than to a 65-room hotel in Manhattan's theater district. Interior designer Jeffrey Bilhuber has erred on the side of eclectic aestheticism. In the mezzanine lounge, Queen Anne chairs abut Brancusi stools and a Fabien Baron mylar mobile offsets vintage framed playbills. Bilhuber's blend of traditional and modern sensibilities is played out with impeccable restraint in the guest rooms. The bathrooms are of chocolate-colored marble and nickel chrome, the walls are finished to simulate hand-corrugated plaster, the furniture is Honduran mahogany, and the selection of quirky ornaments has been distinctively curated. And, lest one should begin to feel it's all about style, the details add a dose of tangible luxury, such as the television with a mirror screen that dissolves once turned on. All of this adds up to a contemporary version of the comfort once provided by the building's original occupant: a 1904 gentlemen's club.

WHARTONESQUE RETREAT

The Inn at Irving Place

56 Irving Place
Rooms from $350

You approach this small, secretive hotel – formed by the joining of two 1830s townhouses – by a flight of steep steps from the sidewalk to the parlor floor. To the left as you enter is Lady Mendl's, an antique-furnished tea salon serving a five-course high tea with sandwiches of the thinly-sliced cucumber-and-smoked-salmon variety. The dozen atmospheric guest rooms, restored by owner Naomi Blumenthal with Larry Wente in 1994, feature fireplaces (non-working, unfortunately, but there is a blazing fire in the parlor during winter months) and hardwood floors. They are furnished with period armoires, four-poster brass beds, Oriental rugs and antique lighting fixtures. While some have likened the experience of the Inn to a sojourn with one's eccentric great-aunt, the bed and breakfast has far more romantic potential than such a comparison evokes. The Madame Olenska suite – named in homage to Edith Wharton, who once lived in nearby Gramercy Square – is the largest in the hotel. It boasts a window seat overlooking Irving Place, an antique typewriter and a sitting room in which to take your complimentary continental breakfast and *The New York Times,* or to receive visitors. Every bathroom features an early 20th-century pedestal sink and brass fixtures. And though such luxury might tempt you to stay in your claw-foot tub with a copy of *The Age of Innocence*, observation of more contemporary manners can be found a short walk in any direction from the inn's front door. A few blocks to the southwest is Union Square, originally constructed in 1831 and now home to the bustling Greenmarket above ground, and a major subway hub below. Take the L train three stops towards Brooklyn to explore the city's hippest neighborhood and most vibrant emerging art scene, Williamsburg.

Hotel on Rivington

`52`

`1`

107 Rivington Street
Rooms from $255

This striking new hotel is certainly not trying to blend in with its surroundings. The 21-story gleaming glass edifice towers above the 19th-century tenements that characterize the determinedly bohemian Lower East Side. Brainchild of real estate developer Paul Stallings, the hotel has attracted a lot of attention — certainly for its incongruity, but also for the bold design statement that it makes both inside and out. Young architect duo Grzywinski Pons is responsible for the tinted glass and zinc shingle exterior. The interior is a composite of the work of several prominent designers, including Marcel Wanders, who has created a sculptural entrance that resembles the curvaceous interior of an igloo, and India Mahdavi, who produced the guest room furnishings. Each of the 110 rooms is somewhat larger than your average New York hotel room. This sense of spaciousness is only enhanced by the floor-to-ceiling windows offering views of lower Manhattan and — on the higher floors — beyond. The rooms are designed to make the most of the urban scenery; wake-up calls, for instance, trigger motorized curtains that slide open to reveal the view. In the bathroom, the shower stall abuts the building's exterior window. Guests with less exhibitionist tendencies will be glad to hear that the designers have also installed an optional conceal-and-reveal device in the window. The bathrooms also feature decadent, oversized Japanese soaking tubs and deliciously heated mosaic Bisazza floor tiles. If you can bear to leave your tub, the second-floor lounge, facing onto the fashionable thoroughfare of Rivington Street, provides an elegant setting in which to read the papers over an espresso. Designer Pierro Lissoni is responsible for such details as the deep ebony wood and beautiful Venini chandelier.

A treat awaits guests of the Sixty Thompson: its rooftop terrace offers a breathtaking panorama of Manhattan's skyline, toothed with water towers in the foreground. The view stretches as far as the Empire State Building to the north, and across the Hudson River to New Jersey to the west. The hotel's owners, The Pomeranc Group, had to buy the air rights from all the neighboring buildings for their 13-story hotel to pass local zoning laws. Steve Jacobs, one of the pioneers of the 1980s vogue for SoHo and TriBeCa loft and industrial building conversions, was the architect and Thomas O'Brien, of Aero Studios, the interior designer. O'Brien, whose clients include Giorgio Armani and Ralph Lauren, took his inspiration for this hotel from disparate sources, including the marble floor of a reflecting pool in Pompeii, a 1942 photograph of Burt Lancaster reclining on a long sofa in his Malibu house, and the 1930s minimalism of French interior designer Jean-Michel Frank. Visitors approach the hotel, which is between Spring and Broome Streets and nicely off SoHo's center, through a recessed courtyard planted with white birches. A downstairs entrance foyer introduces the recurring color palette of brown, grey and red, and ushers guests upward to the light-filled reception area and to the adjoining bar and lounge on the second floor, scene of many a fashion shoot and celebrity interview. The focus of each guest room is the platform bed that extends from a full-wall leather headboard. The cerused wood furniture includes a sofa, a high-backed Thompson Chair (based on an English Déco chaise O'Brien found in London), and a dark wood table arrangement to replace the traditional hotel desk. The 2,000-square-foot (185-square-meter) duplex penthouse loft with a four-poster king-sized bed and two private garden decks is the jewel in the hotel's crown.

The Lowell

1 28 East 63rd Street

Rooms from $445

Scandinavian down comforters, Chinese porcelains, 18th-century prints, Fauchon and Dean & Deluca goodies in the minibars, and Bulgari amenities in the marble bathrooms – the guest rooms of The Lowell exude uptown luxury from every Frette linen pore. The suites, boasting wood fires, libraries and terraces, are even more sumptuous. Its discreet location on tree-lined East 63rd Street in the Upper East Side Historic District and its immaculate service endear this hotel to a privacy-seeking clientele. Originally an apartment hotel of one- and two-bedroom suites, designed in the late 1920s by Henry Stern Churchill, The Lowell is now a landmark building. The exterior of the lower floors features a mosaic façade of brick and glazed terracotta; higher up is a series of asymmetrical terraced setbacks. The gorgeous lobby, designed by Dalmar Tift III, is comprised of Art Déco details, French Empire-style furniture, chiaroscuro walls and a rare desk console signed by Edgar Brandt. The slightly too exquisite chintz of the hotel's furnishings may not suit all tastes, but if you like your country cottages one block from Central Park and within walking distance of all the uptown museums and Madison Avenue boutiques, this will be your whimsical nirvana.

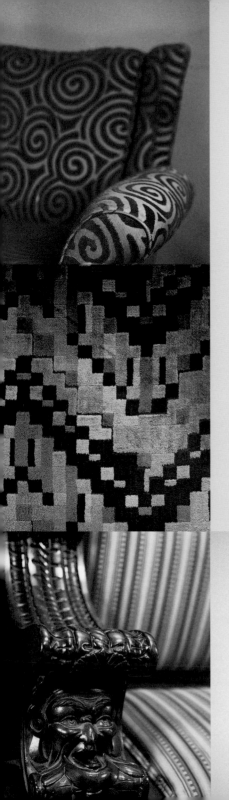

34 **Hotel Chelsea**
21 222 West 23rd Street
Rooms from $150

Legends of the Chelsea loom even larger than the imposing Victorian–Gothic edifice that dominates much of the block between Seventh and Eighth Avenues on 23rd Street. Apart from the more dramatic scenes that have colored its rooms and corridors, such as Nancy Spungen's stabbing at the hands of boyfriend Sid Vicious in room 100 and Dylan Thomas's last drink in 205, the hotel's guest register is a veritable index of 20th-century American literature. Long-term tenants have included Mark Twain, Tennessee Williams, Arthur Miller and O. Henry; Arthur Clarke penned *2001: A Space Odyssey* and William Burroughs wrote *Naked Lunch* within its walls. But the hotel's location in the gallery district of the city and its residents, including Jim Dine, Claes Oldenburg and Warhol's Chelsea Girls, have earned it the dubious distinction of being named the sleeping quarters for the art world – albeit for those with a rock-and-roll- rather than MoMA-inspired interpretation of art. Holly Solomon has a gallery in room 425 and the lobby doubles as a gallery showing the work of previous residents, some of whom purportedly paid for their lodging in kind. Since 2001, a far less down-and-out clientele can be found under the hotel's canopy as they line up for entrance to velvet-roped Serena, a swanky subterranean cocktail bar named for its owner, a well-known New York caterer. The Chelsea's red-brick façade and lacy wrought-iron balconies are the work of Hubert Pirsson & Co. who built the hotel in 1884 as the city's first co-operative apartment complex. Be warned that seedy cool is apt to teeter dangerously on the edge of downright dingy. But if, like Leonard Cohen, writer of the song "Chelsea Hotel #2," you "love hotels to which, at 4 a.m., you can bring along a midget, a bear and four ladies, drag them to your room and no one cares about it at all," then you'll feel at right at home.

34 **Hotel Gansevoort**

25 18 Ninth Avenue
Rooms from $435

The Meatpacking District was until recently an area frequented primarily by meat wholesalers in bloody aprons and transvestite prostitutes. The fact that it now has two hotels (with New York's first Standard Hotel in the pipeline) is testament to the area's newly acquired, and irreversible, status as a desirable retail, restaurant and nightlife destination. What the Gansevoort has to offer over its neighboring competitors, such as the New York outpost of London members' club Soho House, is its roof. Never mind securing an outside table at Pastis or a spot in the VIP lounge at Hiro, one of the best places to be in the MPD is 14 stories above the still-pungent cobbled streets and sidewalks, inhaling the Hudson River breezes. In response to what he saw as the lack of good rooftop spaces in the city, architect Stephen B. Jacobs made the hotel's roof the signature feature of the Gansevoort. Visit the landscaped garden, Plunge Pool Bar and 45-foot long, glass-encased and heated swimming pool, and you'll quickly become a believer. The views over lower Manhattan and across the Hudson are unparalleled, it's often quiet, and the underwater music and lighting is not as Miami Vice as you would think. The Gansevoort's 187 rooms are spacious, each with nine-foot ceilings, many with bay windows, and about a third of them with glass-sheathed balconies. Andi Pepper's interiors are minimalist but comfortable, using a muted color palette in combination with opulent fabrics and materials. Luxuries on tap include multi-line cordless phones, plasma and LCD televisions, complimentary Wi-Fi access throughout the hotel, and 400-thread count Fili d'Oro linens on the beds.

eat

There are some 130 eateries per Manhattan square mile (2.5 square kilometers) that represent every conceivable national and regional cuisine the world has to offer — along with curious fusions of more than one of them — available any time of the day or night. New York is a city that eats out in all variety of manners, two recent trends being reinvigorated interpretations of hotel dining and New American, which celebrates down-home ingredients inventively (sometimes wildly) prepared. Striking décor isn't hard to find, so this selection identifies those places that offer exceptional cuisine or an enduring, often quiet sense of style: places that simply feel good to eat out in.

SMOKED FIS

PRICE PER 1/4 LB

STURGEON	12.00	Whi
Pastrami Salmon or Gravlox	8.75	Whole
Eastern Nova Scotia Salmon	8.75	Center
Western Nova Scotia Salmon	8.25	Jumbo
Belly (Salty) Lox	6.75	Chubs
Kippered (Baked) Salmon	6.75	Rain
Sable	8.75	Impo

Barney Greengrass Sturgeon King

541 Amsterdam Avenue

This Jewish delicatessen, established at this location in 1927 when the Greengrass family moved their business from Harlem, provides the perfect environment in which to get a smoked-fish taste of Upper West Side life. The interior and the attitude have been cured as perfectly as their specialty sturgeon. The counters burst with three varieties of Russian caviar, smoked rainbow brook trout, pickled herrings, kippered salmon, chopped liver, pastrami and bialys. The atmosphere is that of an old diner with fluorescent lighting, and faded Formica wainscoting and vinyl are the materials of choice. Upper West Side families, writers and desiccated but immaculately turned-out old timers come here on Saturday mornings for eggs scrambled with nova and onions washed down with cream soda. You'll feel privileged to join them.

COMFORT FOOD
52 Freeman's

21 2 Freeman Alley

Follow the stream of hungover Lower East Siders to this
elusive unmarked restaurant at the end of a blind alley off
Rivington Street, and tuck into a morning-after Bloody
Mary and plate of eggs. Once inside, diners have the
impression of having stumbled into a Highland hunting
lodge. The dark walls are appointed with loops of greenery,
age-spotted mirrors, old prints and stuffed ducks fastened
mid-flight above the fireplace. The staff, casual with their
just-out-of-bed hairdos and still-in-bed outfits, will find you
a place at one of the wooden tables, set simply with candles
and jam jars of wild flowers. Morning visitors are soothed
by 1920s jazz music and the hiss of steaming milk. Owner
and architect Taavvo Somer's menu features such 1950s
throwbacks as Devils on Horseback (piping-hot Stilton-
stuffed prunes, wrapped in bacon), wild boar terrine with
lingonberry sauce, and venison stew with kumquats and
white beans. For dessert, there are stewed plums or apple
Brown Betty with vanilla ice cream.

DINER STYLE

94 Diner

4 85 Broadway, Brooklyn

Diner, at the epicenter of ultra-hip Williamsburg, is an uncontested mecca of cool. Ever since co-owners Andrew Tarlow and Mark Firth refurbished this battered 1927 dining car in 1999, artists and fashionistas from an ever-increasing radius have colonized its leaning banquettes on Sunday mornings or late Friday nights, to view themselves and each other nonchalantly in the bar-length strip of mirror. The music is loud – there's a DJ on weekend evenings – and the mullet-haired staff have just the right mix of friendliness and reserve. With its wobbly bar stools, cracked mosaic flooring and bunches of fresh flowers on the bar, Diner manages to retain an indefinable essence of run-down charm. The plastic-clad menu lists its good-value foods generically – "green salad," "spinach" or "burger" – in suitably basic Courier font. Wielding ballpoint pens, the waiting staff will scrawl Caroline Fidanza's specials, such as perfectly cooked whole trout or codfish hash, on your table's paper covering.

94 Peter Luger's Steakhouse

5 178 Broadway, Brooklyn

The favored way to arrive at this infamous Brooklyn steak house is by limousine. Fur coats and fat wallets congregate daily to gorge what is generally deemed to be the best porterhouse steak in the country. The 1887 eatery, originally called Charles Luger's Café, Billiard and Bowling Alley and patronized by local shipyard workers, was purchased in 1950 by Sol Forman, a regular customer who owned a metalworking plant across the street; his descendants still run the place. Veteran waiters gruffly play their parts in a no-nonsense yet consciously theatrical dining experience. Menus are reserved for first-timers only, and knives, forks, plates and napkins are flung rather than placed on the bare oak tables. It is the Iowa corn-fed beef, however, that is the star performer of the show. Sizzling shortloins, dry-aged on the premises, are served for two, three or four on platters ritualistically tilted so that the waiter can spoon a mixture of butter and meat juices over your chunks of tender meat. The only way to leave Peter Luger's is sated.

14 **Megu**
6 62 Thomas Street

Megu, meaning "blessing" in Japanese, is the US debut of Japan's unstoppable restaurateur, Koji Imai. A team of 25 chefs presents contemporary Japanese cuisine, including *sumibi aburiyaki*, which is grilled using *bincho-tan*, a charcoal imported from Kyoto and prized for its purifying properties. In both Japan and the US, Imai works directly with farmers and fishermen, and local organic producers. Architect Yasumichi Morita created the spectacular two-tiered space, blending contemporary design with traditional Japanese references, such as the giant temple bell (*bonsho*) suspended from the ceiling, and the ice sculpture of a Buddha, carved each afternoon. The 205-seat dining room is overlooked by the upper-level bar, which hosts frequent sake-tasting parties. A compromise between transparency and privacy is achieved by the walls of interlocking rice bowls and sake vases. White leather banquettes with soaring backs provide an intimate dining backdrop for such dishes as Kobe beef, grilled at the table on river stones, and foie gras teriyaki skewers.

34 **Corner Bistro**
41 331 West 4th Street

BEER AND BURGERS

It's 2 a.m., you're with friends and have had a few drinks, and your mind is firmly fixed upon the idea of a burger. Your course is set for this dark and divey sports bar, where cheeseburgers and chicken sandwiches served on paper plates with all the essential condiments cost $4 and $5.50 respectively. The jukebox is well stocked with mournful music, and McSorley's ale is only $2 a glass. Style and Corner Bistro are words that do not sit easily together – the clientele is regrettably of the frat boy variety – but this atmospheric corner tavern, located in the far reaches of the West Village where the street grid system breaks down most fully, is a great place to watch a game or simply nurse a bourbon on the rocks at the bar to the tune of Tom Waits.

OYSTER VAULT

66
3 **The Grand Central Oyster Bar & Restaurant**

Grand Central Station, Lower Concourse, 42nd Street

Don't be put off by the early 1980s rainbow graphics on the door; this place is timeless. Lunchtimes are best. A canny waitress will slide fresh biscuits and butter at you the minute you pick a white leatherette seat at one of the U-shaped counters and serve your food in the blink of an eye. But take your time and soak it all in, including the recently cleaned Guastavino vaulted ceilings, tiled floor and enormous paper menu of oysters, harvested from all over North America and now being shucked in big tubs at a side bar. The clientele includes few travelers, but most tourists choose the blander fast-food concessions on the food court above. Instead the Oyster Bar is the lunchtime refuge of Midtown businessmen and quintessential New York characters who'll "take the usual, please, Jeannie," whether that's a clam chowder, an oyster pan roast or a dozen Blue Points.

BRIGHT LIGHTS, BIG CITY

14 **Odeon**
5 145 West Broadway

The 1930s substructure of this restaurant interior is still visible after a 1980 renovation at the hands of fraternal restaurant stylists Brian and Keith McNally and owner Lynn Wagenknecht. Original fixtures such as the granite floor, the Art Déco wood paneling and pendant globe lights remain. As Jay McInerney understates in *Bright Lights, Big City*, the Odeon "makes you feel reasonable at any hour, often against bad odds." The afternoon brings daylight, severed into strips by Venetian blinds, to a Bloody Mary brunch and the small hours see a lively crew of fashionistas and art types crowded into red and black leather banquettes for good American bistro fare.

VENETIAN TRATTORIA

106 Al di La

4 248 Fifth Avenue, Brooklyn

The fact that no reservations are taken at this stylish Italian trattoria, and that big shots arriving in limos have to wait for a table just as long as you do, sets a delicious tone for the evening. Sampling the fine Italian wine list in the downstairs bar and sniffing the tantalizing smells emanating from chef Anna Klinger's kitchen will keep you entertained while you wait for a space in the dining room. Al di La's feeling of casual elegance is a composite of cracked floor tiles, a single glass chandelier hanging from an eroded silver pressed-tin ceiling, mismatched china, and the chatty hospitality of proprietor Emiliano Coppa. Summer evening light fills the whole room, and in winter displays of seasonal fare like pumpkins and a heavy velvet curtain around the door keep things cozy. Arrive hungry so you can try the baccala mantecato (salt cod beaten with olive oil and served on grilled polenta), followed by homemade ravioli filled with red beets and ricotta, melted butter and poppy seeds, braised rabbit (a classic Northern Italian dish), along with a dessert of pear cake with bitter chocolate chunks. Perfetto.

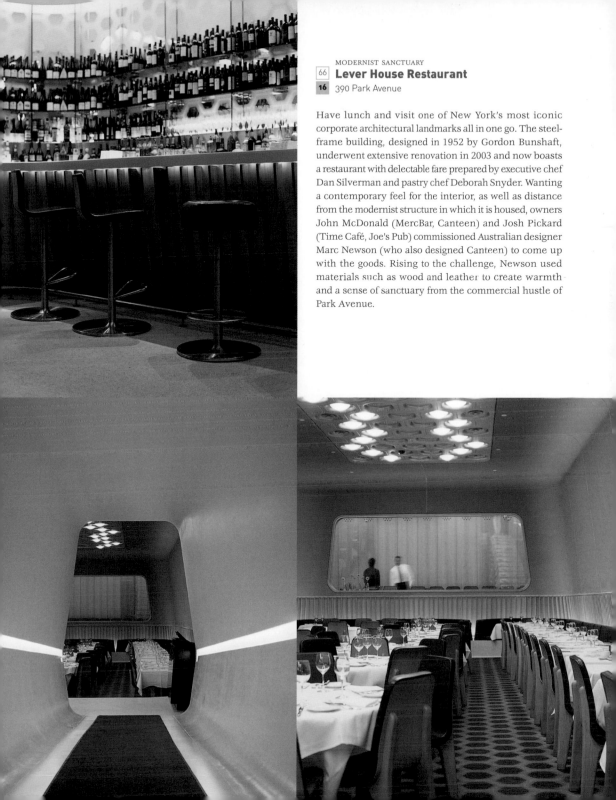

66 Lever House Restaurant

16 390 Park Avenue

Have lunch and visit one of New York's most iconic corporate architectural landmarks all in one go. The steel-frame building, designed in 1952 by Gordon Bunshaft, underwent extensive renovation in 2003 and now boasts a restaurant with delectable fare prepared by executive chef Dan Silverman and pastry chef Deborah Snyder. Wanting a contemporary feel for the interior, as well as distance from the modernist structure in which it is housed, owners John McDonald (MercBar, Canteen) and Josh Pickard (Time Café, Joe's Pub) commissioned Australian designer Marc Newson (who also designed Canteen) to come up with the goods. Rising to the challenge, Newson used materials such as wood and leather to create warmth and a sense of sanctuary from the commercial hustle of Park Avenue.

52

Jack's Luxury Oyster Bar

16 246 East 5th Street

The husband-and-wife owners of sushi restaurant Jewel Bako have created another gem of a restaurant, this time right across the street and occupying the first two floors of their own East Village carriage house. The ground floor holds a mere four tables for à la carte sampling. Another intimate room reserved for the tasting menu is found up a steep, carpeted staircase. The details were chosen to evoke a 19th-century seaside hotel: red-checked wallpaper, silver toast racks and candlesticks, horn-handled knives, and even a porcelain King Charles spaniel. The meal begins with a dish of peppered and sugared pecans and an amuse bouche of foie gras and caramelized onion on white corn bread, followed by bisque and three-tiered platters of seafood, including such oysters as Fanny Bay and Chef Creek from the West Coast, and Malpeque and Cheda Butto from the East, and dishes like seared foie gras on a bed of sweet lentils. Now and again Jack himself, besuited, bespectacled and spiky-haired, will be spotted clutching a bottle of wine and a gold-embossed menu, dashing across the street like the time-pressed White Rabbit.

I'LL HAVE WHAT SHE'S HAVING
52 **Katz's Delicatessen**
20 205 East Houston Street

A stalwart institution of the Jewish Lower East Side since 1888, Katz's Delicatessen is the place to satisfy your cravings for hot pastrami and corned-beef sandwiches. Favored by presidents – even Bill Clinton's famously large appetite was apparently satiated after a sandwich (plus two more to take back to Washington) – it is also popular among actors. Meg Ryan famously demonstrated her fake orgasm in *When Harry Met Sally* at one of Katz's Formica tables. The air is thick with the smell of hanging salamis and pickles, and the bustle of regulars who handle the obstacle course necessary to obtain a sandwich with wisecracking ease.

52 Craft
5 43 East 19th Street

Diners can literally craft their own meals at this innovative New American restaurant. Tom Colicchio's refreshingly back-to-basics approach to cooking puts some of the onus on the diner. You have to choose whether you want your meat, fish or vegetables to be roasted, braised or sautéed, and which of the side dishes – large and served family-style in copper pots and casseroles – you'd like to complement them. The interior of Craft glows. Warmth emanates from large, cherry-wood tables, and the soft light of orange-filament Ferrowatt bulbs is reflected from the imbuia wood floor. Inspired by his collection of brass objects designed by Carl Aubock, Craft's interior designer Peter Bentels chose bronze for the front door, bathroom sinks and interior metal accents – a welcome respite from the hard-edged aluminum and cool stainless steel of too many restaurant interiors of the past few years.

CAFÉ CULTURE
14 Café Gitane
18 242 Mott Street

Beautiful people – lots of them – gather at Café Gitane, so expect a long line. And while the calculated insouciance of the young Italian photographer at the next table, showing contact sheets to an Austrian art director, can be a little grating, you'll forgive and forget as soon as you settle into this delightful café. With a delicate Moroccan glass of fresh mint tea in hand and a towering sandcastle of couscous to come, you can lean back amid the eddy of NoLIta activity and bask in the afternoon sun streaming in across the tiled floor.

Public is the joint creation of design and concept group AvroKO, head chef Brad Farmerie, and consulting chefs Peter Gordon and Anna Hansen from London's The Providores. Their menu is bold and multicultural, combining the flavors and produce of New Zealand and Australia with Middle Eastern and Asian influences. One favorite starter is kangaroo and coriander falafel, with a lemon-tahini sauce and green pepper relish, and entrées include a concoction of monkfish cheeks, mussels and cockles, served with courgette ribbons and lemon-braised fennel. Industrial materials have been used for the interior, including concrete and rough white brick, offset by rich wooden floors and soft light emanating from the glass oil lamps converted from soap dispensers. Post office boxes lining the entryway, menus printed on pale yellow manila files and presented on clipboards, and bathroom doors with frosted glass and gold beveled numbers, salvaged from an old school, continue the utilitarian aesthetic.

drink

New York runs on two liquid fuels. By day, the steam that leaks through its manholes seems to come from some giant subterranean espresso machine fixing the city's inhabitants with its nerve-jangling energy. Towards day's end, it is the cocktails that provide the high: Gimlets, Gibsons, Cosmopolitans, Manhattans, Highballs, French 75s — the very names ooze nostalgia. Measures don't exist and the art of mixology is highly evolved. Imbibing in New York is a specialized activity, with particular bars for particular beverages, moods and times of the day or night. And the nights can be long: most bars stay open until 4 a.m.

52
29

Good World Barber Shop

3 Orchard Street

When this Swedish-run bar in a former Chinese barbershop
opened it seemed impossibly far away from the action.
The interior is spare, with industrial-grade floors and plain
wooden tables and only a large moose head on the wall
behind the bar for decoration. Climb on one of the tall
barstools for a mean Aquavit martini and bar snacks, such
as toast skagen made of white fish roe and Norwegian
shrimp in a light lemon dill and sour-cream sauce, served
on a toasted sourdough baguette or salmon rolls. DJs play
most nights of the week and there is a small yard out back.

52
22

Teany

90 Rivington Street

With 90 blends of tea, some harder alternatives such as
Champagne mojitos and sangria, a mod all-white, glass and
chrome interior and tunes mixed by the musician himself,
you don't have to abstain from much to enjoy Moby's
vegetarian sanctuary. The artist also known as Melville
Hall is a hands-off owner, leaving the menu choices and
the day-to-day running of the café to his partner and fellow
vegan, Kelly Tisdale.

BEER, SPIT AND SAWDUST

52 McSorley's Old Ale House

15 15 East 7th Street

"There is a thick musty smell that acts as a balm to jerky nerves; it is really a rich compound of the smells of pine sawdust, tap drippings, pipe tobacco, coal smoke, and onions." So wrote Joseph Mitchell in his 1942 book *McSorley's Wonderful Saloon*. These days the best time to visit this venerable institution is the afternoon, when shafts of sunlight slice through the dense atmosphere and you can banter with the Irish barkeeps. First opened in 1854, it took 116 years for McSorley's to allow women across the threshold.

CALIFORNIAN THEME PARK

34 **The Park**

26 118 Tenth Avenue

Nightlife impresarios Sean McPherson (Bar Marmont in L.A.) and Eric Goode (New York's B-Bar, see p. 158) hired design guru Jim Walrod to conceive their latest restaurant and lounge. They took three taxi garages and turned them into an enormous theme park whose interior references country lodge and opium den in equal measure. A Dracaena tree, gold-dipped Mies van der Rohe Barcelona chairs, giant benches cut from tree trunks, and crackling fires all add their own notes and contribute to a rare oasis in an industrial West Chelsea setting.

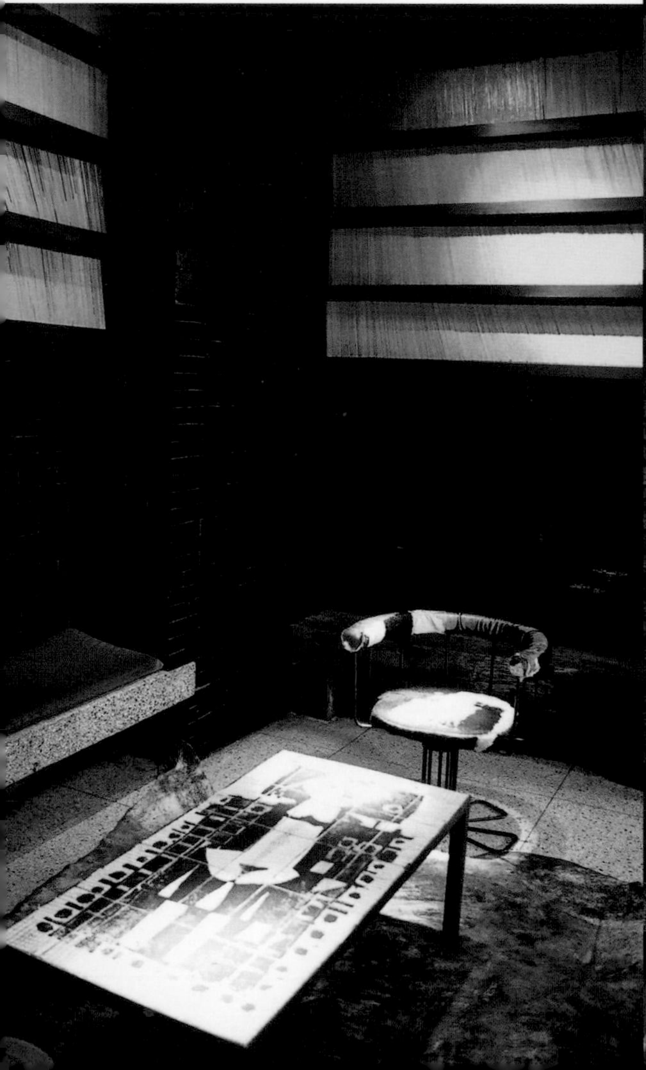

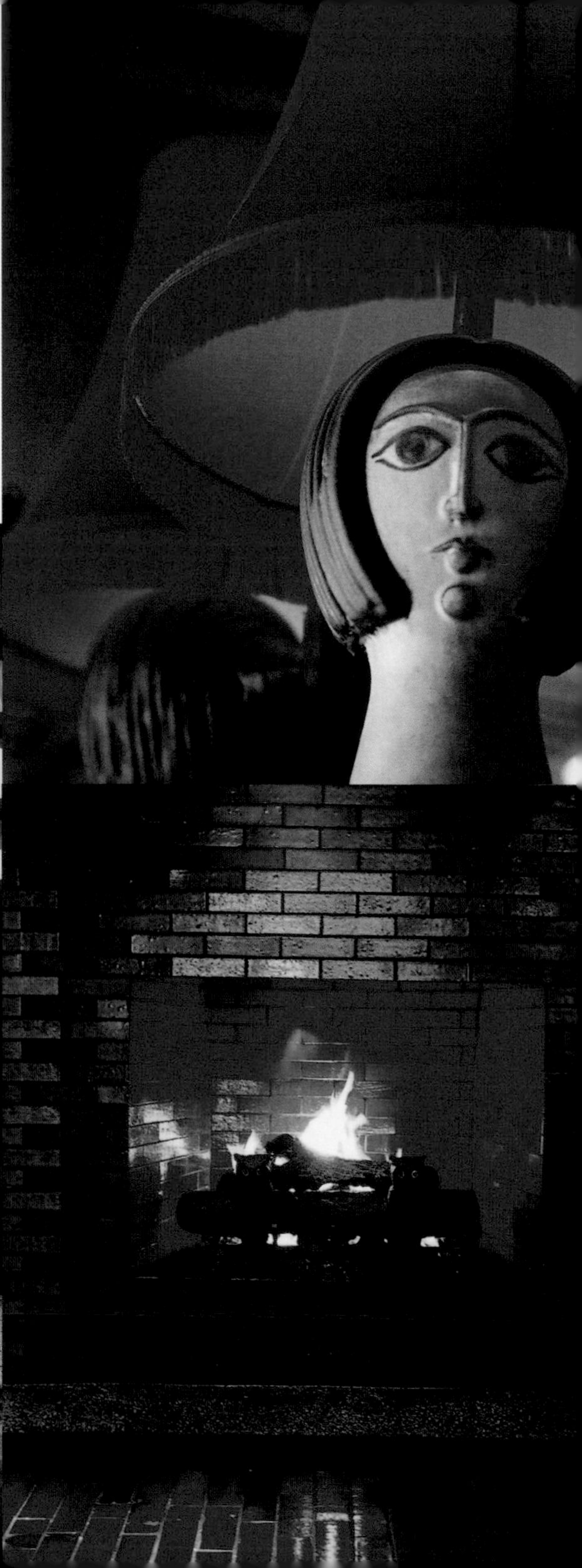

After outfitting many of Manhattan's better-known French bistros, Bernard Decanali opened a café of his own in his Boerum Hill antiques shop. In the summer the leafy garden, with its eclectic assortment of seating and old enamel advertising signage, is a great place for a few bottles of wine and fantastic snacking fare. Inside, the crazy collection of objects – such as stuffed crocodiles, 1950s hatstands and chandeliers, stacked Parisian salon–style from floor to ceiling – combines with a clientele that easily mixes families and local hipsters.

14 **13** **Caffé Roma**

385 Broome Street

A thimble-full of strong espresso and a Sicilian-style cannoli from one of Little Italy's oldest pasticcerias are the perfect refreshments on a New York Saturday afternoon. Sit at a marble-topped table near the window and watch the bustle go by. Relics of late 19th-century Little Italy, such as the pressed-tin ceiling, a saloon clock that hangs over the espresso machine, and the wood-backed bar behind the take-away pastry counter, remain undisturbed thanks to the long-time family running of the business.

34 **22** **Passerby**

436 West 15th Street

Fortunately, this bar's regulars have managed to defend it against the attacks of marauding "bridge-and-tunnelers," so it is still possible to lean on the long bar with artists from gallery owner Gavin Brown's celebrated stable (p. 17), including Elizabeth Peyton and Udomsak Krisanamis. The room's raw interior, designed by artist Mark Handforth, features a bar made from wood that furniture designer George Nakashima had, before he died, intended for a dining table. A multi-colored disco floor by Piotr Uklanski pulses to the beat of some of the city's best DJs.

66 King Cole Bar & Lounge

13 St. Regis Hotel, 2 East 55th Street

Legend has it that this dark and magical bar tucked off the lobby of the swanky St. Regis hotel is the birthplace of the Bloody Mary, which here goes by its original name, the Red Snapper. After a couple of these potent, spicy concoctions, accompanied by liberal servings of salted almonds and macadamia nuts, you will feel that you are, like the eponymous nursery-rhyme hero of the bar's spectacular mural by Maxfield Parrish, a "merry old soul." The wood-paneled warmth and the deep banquettes provide refuge from the crowds of Fifth Avenue.

14 Chibi's Sake Bar

30 238 Mott Street

Chibi's proprietor, Marja Samsom, named the bar after her French bulldog, who likes to lounge in a corner of the main room and can be seen on special occasions skateboarding on the sidewalk outside. Bar staff will help you distinguish an Umenishiki from a Nanbu Toji when it comes time to choose your sake, and will advise on the relative merits of a Chibitini versus a Saketini. Snacks include Japanese delicacies, Kumamoto oysters and mushroom dumplings This is a laid-back drinking den, good for small groups late at night.

CLANDESTINE COCKTAILS
52 **Angel's Share**
13 8 Stuyvesant Street

It is a combination of strict house rules – no standing, no groups of more than four, no shouting – and an out-of-the-way location at the rear of a second-floor fluorescent-lit Japanese restaurant that helps screen the crowds at this jewel of a bar. For even more privacy, seek out the curtained-off section at the end of the narrow space. The old-school cocktails are mixed with cool precision by some of the most skilled bartenders in town. Named for the portion of alcohol that's lost to the "angels" during the ageing process, this bar breathes nothing but refinement.

The Bohemian Hall and Beer Garden was built in 1910 by the Bohemian Citizens' Benevolent Society for Astoria's transplanted population of Czechs. Members of this fraternal society who had day jobs as masons, plumbers and electricians volunteered their services to construct the hall, and transformed a patch of Long Island farmland into an authentic European beer garden. At one time there were more than 800 such beer gardens in New York, but today this is the only that one survives. Spend a leisurely summer evening in this garden that with its picnic tables, bandstand, and trees hung with bunting has the feel of an Eastern European village square. The drink of choice here is Pilsner Urqell by the pint, and barbeque stations cater to your kielbasa and sauerkraut cravings. You may even end up dancing to the strident tunes of a Slovak folkband.

In its former life Brooklyn Social was an Italian men's social club, and the bar retains enough original features to create a suitably sociable mood, but not so many that it enters the dreaded theme-bar territory. A recessed area with an armchair and chandelier, delightfully labeled as the Ladies' Auxiliary Lounge, together with subdued jazz music, sepia photographs of former club members, a red pressed-tin ceiling and revolving ceiling fans add to the clubby feel. Deadpan evocations of restraint continue at the bar. Bartenders wear ties, hair pomade and aprons, and take care over the preparation of cocktails like Matt's Ginger Old-Fashioned (bourbon, ginger, sugar, cherries, orange and soda) and the Society Riposto (vodka, tangerine slices and fresh rosemary). There's a porch at the back for smokers, and during the summer months tables and folding chairs are set up in the astro-turfed garden, hung with bunting streamers.

INTIMATE TERMS
66 **Single Room Occupancy**
31 360 West 53rd Street

This speakeasy in the basement of an off-the-beaten-path Midtown brownstone is barely announced by the glow of a green sconce. Locating the space and buzzing the buzzer are the only credentials you'll need to join the distinctly non-Midtown crowd sipping wine and beer in a dimly lit bare-bones interior. The railroad-style room glows faintly from the frosted light tiles in the celing and floor, which illuminate the hordes of beautiful people who come here to groove to the thumpingly loud music.

EIGHTIES GLAM SCENE
14 **B-Bar & Grill**
63 40 East 4th Street

There is a scene in John Waters's 1998 film *Pecker* in which a young provincial photographer, discovered by an avaricious gallery owner, is heralded at a dinner by the New York art scene. The dinner takes place at the Bowery Bar – the perfect location for Waters's satirical portrait of the city's art-world élite. The bar and its rainbow light-bedecked patio was once a gas station on the city's most famously down-and-out street. Converted in the 1980s by Eric Goode and Serge Becker, it now hosts club-nights, including "Beige," Erich Conrad's celebrity-studded gay extravaganza.

CHURCH OF VODKA
Temple Bar
14
68 332 Lafayette Street

Like some strange clue in an Indiana Jones movie, the silhouette of an iguana skeleton on the wall at 332 Lafayette Street is the Temple Bar's only marker. Inside, the plush dark interior, magnificent cherry-oak bar, black marble and dim Art Déco sconces are seductively enveloping. Try one of a massive collection of vodkas with a bowl of spicy popcorn, or choose from a bar menu that includes fresh oysters on the half shell, Beluga caviar, salmon canapés and Angus steak skewers. Then try to leave. You'll find that time has its own measure in this alcohol-hazed shrine.

shop

From the gargantuan department stores of Madison Avenue to the waif-sized boutiques that cluster along Elizabeth, Rivington, Perry, Bond Streets and Bedford Avenue, or wherever the breeze of fashion blows them, New York provides the material — both raw and ready-to-wear — from which entire lifestyles can be assembled. As the selection below attests, a rich spectrum of retail experiences awaits: classics; shops where the interiors are as fashionable as the wares they house; and a new variety that blends the essences of shop, gallery and museum. Prepare to be pleasantly confused.

80 **Barneys**

2 660 Madison Avenue

At this axis of New York style (with the most decadent of Christmastime window displays in town), you'll indulge in a truly luxurious shopping experience that spans nine floors displaying thousands of products and ends with lunch and top-quality people-watching at Fred's restaurant on the basement level. Minimalist architect Peter Marino was commissioned in 1993 by the Pressman family to convert the 1955 building at Madison Avenue and 61st Street into the 230,000 square feet (21,350 square meters) of unmissable New York event that Barneys is today.

UPTOWN BARGAINS DOWNTOWN

34 **Barneys Co-op**

10 236 West 18th Street
116 Wooster Street

The downtown branches of the uptown department store carry such labels as Daryl K, Katayone Adeli, Jill Stuart and Vivienne Tam, less expensive and more street-inspired than those stocked by their uptown big sister. If you are in the city in August or February, you are in for the fashion spectacle of the Barney's Warehouse Sale, when the 18th Street store slashes prices up to 80 percent. Watch out for the stampede of well-heeled women trying to get to that sexy-secretary Marc Jacobs cashmere cardigan.

94 **ISA**

3 88 North 6th Street, Brooklyn

This modern salon was a welcome arrival to the Williamsburg fashion scene, which, until Isa Saalabi opened shop, was limited solely to vintage and thrift. The concrete space often hosts street-spilling parties for labels such as ORFI, and exhibitions of Brooklyn-grown artists like RoStarr and DJ nights. ISA caters for men with tough denims, sweaters and T-shirts and for women with a good selection of big- and small-name designers (United Bamboo, Marc by Marc Jacobs), local artists (M.R.S.) and hard-to-find pieces (originals from DHBJR).

WELL-HEELED
14 **26**

Sigerson Morrison

26 28 Prince Street

Kari Sigerson's and Miranda Morrison's line of mint-green lined shoes have been a hit with the ladies who lunch ever since they opened their small store in NoLIta eight years ago. The newer, larger location, once a vegetable warehouse, features a storefront grid of aluminum, glass and white "penny tile," which affords enticing views of the luminous interior. Inside, movable brushed-steel tables display their signature kitten-heeled mules and buckled Mary Janes, and a long red banquette designed for Cappellini by Miranda's brother, Jasper.

FASHION SUPERMARKET
14 **53**

Kirna Zabete

53 96 Greene Street

Beth Buccini and Sarah Easley are the minds behind this fascinatingly eclectic SoHo store, which they tout as a "saccharine-free supermarket of style." In 1999 they commissioned Nick Dine to design the rainbow interior, which includes a lavender resin floor, pink uplights and cornflower-blue neoprene seats. With racks loaded with desirable pieces by such designers such as Bruce, Martine Sitbon and Matthew Williamson, this original boutique has garnered a devoted fashion following. There is even a range of designer pet paraphernalia downstairs.

STREET-STYLE GENERAL STORE
Steven Alan

 103 Franklin Street

This TriBeCa emporium of emerging designers was conceived as an old-fashioned general store, with rolling ladders that slide along ceiling-high wooden shelves stacked with La cosa T-shirts and a 1940s pharmacy display case containing Dr. Hauschka cosmetic products. Labels are from the likes of APC, Wink, Martin Margiela 6 and Katayone Adeli. An upholstered bench is flanked by two listening stations whose sample sounds are changed bi-weekly by the people at Other Music (p. 31).

CASING THE JOINT
 Kate Spade Travel

 59 Thompson Street

Number 59 Thompson Street is the location of handbag entrepreneur Kate Spade's very first shop, and its pretty storefront now houses Kate Spade Travel, representing the refined essence of her much-expanded – and phenomenally successful – label. Here you'll find whimsical travel accessories for the modern woman, including hot-water-bottle covers, erasers, colorful notebooks and wallets, vintage scarves and quality luggage in black or striped canvas.

94 **The Future Perfect**

11 115 North 6th Street, Brooklyn

Seattlite David Alhadeff opened the The Future Perfect in Williamsburg to showcase accessories, home furnishings and artwork by up-and-coming designers, many of them from Brooklyn. Much of the work embraces themes of irony and nostalgia, along with a contemporary reinvestigation of decoration. There are several ornamental wallpapers to choose from, and Tobias Wong's "I F*ck for Gucci" limited-edition print is typical of the store's cutting-edge inventory, as is Jason Miller's ceramic Superordinate Antler table lamp. Another thematic undercurrent of the store is sustainability, and many of the products make use of recycled materials. A line of dishware, titled 50¢, is made from vintage dishes that have been reglazed with new patterns, and the Stop It lounge chair is made from black and white rubber stoppers.

When partners Renata Bokalo and Roman Luba opened their pitch-perfect designer lifestyle store in 1999, they also pioneered a retail revolution in the Meatpacking District. The area is now New York's design and fashion Grand Central – much to the bemusement of the few remaining meat packers still operating in the area. Auto features the work of Brooklyn-based designers who manage to combine craftsmanship and knowing modernity in their household objects and accessories: leather flowers by Red Head Amy, stitched pillows by Judy Ross, and much, much more.

Former fashion entrepreneur Murray Moss's white-cube, industrial-design store in SoHo blurs the distinction between museum and shop. The covetable porcelain tableware, crystal and cutlery are presented in thematic association with one another, and contextualized with furniture and lighting. One may find a Hella Jongerius ceramic pot next to a stainless-steel Fisher space pen, next to an Edra pink leather Flap sofa. An adjacent gallery provides in-depth looks at the work of such designer/artists as Tord Boontje and the Campanor Brothers.

14 **Bond 07**

Tunisian-born Selima Salaun has a veritable empire of New York stores featuring her signature quirky sensibility and range of acid-bright eyeglasses. The latest is a gem of a boutique on 25 Prince Street called Lunettes et Chocolat, which takes niche retailing to a delightful extreme by selling only eyeglasses and delicious handmade chocolates. Another of her creations is Le Corset Boutique on 80 Thompson Street, which specializes in gorgeously over-the-top lingerie and loungewear. Bond 07, yet another of her coterie, is situated on NoHo's hip Bond Street (Daryl K and Ghost are among the storefronts that punctuate the brick-and-marble-trimmed row houses and quirky residential lofts). This one-stop shop for stylists focuses on a handpicked selection of accessories, such as hats and vintage Cartier, Rolex and Gucci watches.

Michele Quan and Robin Renzi are jewelry designers who draw their collective inspiration from nature and Middle Eastern themes to make stackable rings, necklaces, bracelets and anklets in silver and gold, using both semiprecious and rare stones and often featuring symbolic carving. This Elizabeth Street store was designed by the New York–based vanguard architectural firm, SHoP. Minimal in design, its one fanfare is a cast-in-place cement basin in the window filled with water and floating flowers.

This emporium of high-end cosmetics and hair and skincare products – the formulae for which have been passed down through the generations since the store opened as an apothecary's in 1851 – is an integral part of New York's heritage. White-lab-coated staff ply you with samples and, using the same plain speaking as the products' no-frills packaging, answer your every beauty-related query. The setting is bizarre: half of the shop houses a collection of vintage motorcycles set on a floral rug before a wall of photographs of customers' babies.

14
48
Prada

575 Broadway

Rem Koolhaas's retail laboratory for Prada arrived in a flurry of media attention in late 2001. Its position at the hub of SoHo and the fact that it runs a whole block means that you can hardly miss it. Its imagination-catching features include the "wave," a concave shape lined with polished zebra wood that runs the length and height of the store; a glass elevator that displays merchandise; and a baroquely wallpapered north wall created by graphic designers, 2 x 4. Groundbreaking technological gadgets abound in this "museum show on indefinite display."

14
35
Jack Spade

56 Greene Street

Spade's signature all-terrain canvas and waxwear bags, jackets and notebooks are presented back-to-back with vintage props such as Braun turntables, *Playboy* magazines, globes and balsa-wood aeroplanes in this 500-square-foot (46-square-meter) SoHo space designed by Stephen Sclaroff. The well-curated collection is the work of Andy Spade (Kate's husband; see p. 165) and might well stand as New York's riposte to Paul Smith.

Seize sur Vingt

243 Elizabeth Street

This loft-style NoLIta store contains a few rolling racks of clean, beautifully cut men's and women's Egyptian cotton button-down shirts and a magnificent Tascam 32 reel-to-reel tape machine. The back third of the store is devoted to the shop's first-rate made-to-measure business. The look of the suits, jackets, trousers and shirts is modern and clean, but husband-and-wife team James and Gwendolyn Jurney use old-world tailoring techniques, such as single-needle stitching for the shirts, and the suits are mostly handsewn.

Marc Jacobs

• 163 Mercer Street (collection ready to wear & men's)
• 385 Bleecker Street (collection accessories & shoes)
• 403–5 Bleecker Street (Marc by Marc Jacobs)

Despite his international success and residence in Paris, Marc Jacobs – who trained at New York's Parsons School of Design – truly belongs to this city. Barneys' painted advertising hoardings once declared "We Love Marc Jacobs," and Manhattan's best-dressed people show no signs of letting their devotion dwindle. These outpost stores were designed by Stephen Jaklitsch and are nestled on the most gorgeous two-block stretch of Bleecker Street (between Bank and Perry Streets) alongside Magnolia Bakery, Lulu Guinness and the flower shop with the beautiful window displays. The company's popular secondary line, Marc by Marc Jacobs, features accessories such as his signature chunky latched and zippered handbags and round-toed, Minnie Mouse-style pumps and flats.

14 **Mayle**

20 252 Elizabeth Street

In an exquisitely assembled boutique in the heart of NoLIta, Brit designer and ex-model Jane Mayle and her gorgeous assistants sell lace dresses and fluttery silk floral blouses that you can pair with librarian-chic leather-edged tweed skirts. Among the racks of this sweet-smelling store – Mayle was responsible for initiating the craze for Votivo red-currant candles – are showcased accessories and other objets d'art such as a Julian Schnabel exhibition poster from 1989. Mayle says her work is inspired by the style of 1950s Italian film star Monica Vitti, whose wardrobe defined feminine elegance. Courtney Love and Sofia Coppola are among the fans of Mayle's off-the-shoulder chemises and crocheted shawls.

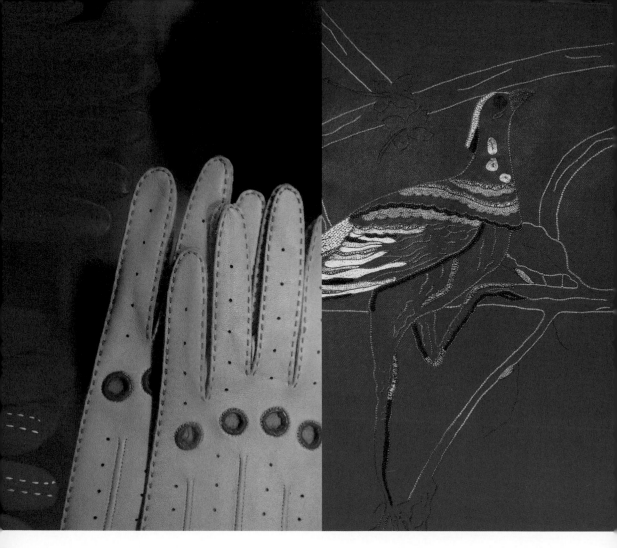

106 **Castor and Pollux**

5 67 ½ Sixth Avenue, Brooklyn

Co-owners Anne-Catherine Lüke and Kerrilynn Hunt are the ladies with the shared vision behind this intimate boutique. Their combined interior design and fashion expertise infuses both the visual character of the store – which they composed themselves from customized fixtures and antiques – and the carefully honed trove of whimsical accessories and clothing that it stows. Clutch wallets by Abas, jewelry by Melissa Joy Manning and a range of classic underwear by On Gossamer are juxtaposed with the kinds of objects that, as they put it, "you would find in one of our apartments." Lüke and Hunt design their own signature line that puts ladylike chic in an urban context. Although the store is situated in a somewhat in-between neighborhood of Brooklyn, it's definitely worth the expedition, especially if you can attend one of the friendly soirées that introduce each new season's collection.

Subterranean boutique I Heart stocks a superb range of girlie clothing from such happening labels as Mary Ping's Slow and Steady Wins the Race and Surface to Air, along with fashionable housewares, like David Wiseman's ceramic-deer hat hangers, and books from the cultish Die Gestalten Verlag. Owners Antonia Kojuharova and Jill Bradshaw also curate a series of exhibitions by graphic artists for those less inclined to part with their cash.

Afer a trundle round the Museum of Modern Art and its fabulous bar (p. 69), you'll also appreciate Richard Gluckman's retail spaces found throughout the museum. On the first floor, MoMA Design and Book Store features books, art reproductions and design objects, and an exhibition shop on the sixth floor showcases products related to temporary exhibitions, further blurring the distinction between museum and retail experience.

retreat

New Yorkers know that weekend-long releases from the pressure of the city are essential for their long-term survival. Luckily for the time-deficient – visitors and residents alike – a mere 100-mile (160-kilometer) radius of Manhattan encompasses a topographical variety with ample potential for both active and contemplative diversion: from the sea-level shenanigans of the Hamptons to the high-altitude hippy hangouts of the Catskill Mountains, from the history-rich rolling pastures of Bucks County in Pennsylvania to the art-world destination found in the deep wooded valley carved by the Hudson River.

Catskills: A Countercultural Escape

- Storm King Art Center
- Café Tamayo
- The Villa at Saugerties

The Catskill Mountains is a spectacular wilderness, which, with Woodstock as its unofficial capital, is the counterculture's retreat of choice. The area has also caught the attention of those New Yorkers recently priced out of the Hamptons and now casting about for an alternative Arcadia. To join them, from Manhattan, take the George Washington Bridge to the Palisades Parkway North for a scenic drive up the west bank of the Hudson River. Make a stop at Storm King Art Center, a magnificent sculpture park that ranges over 500 acres (200 hectares) of landscaped lawns, fields and woodlands ornamented by monumental pieces by postwar American and European artists such as Alexander Calder, David Smith and Andy Goldsworthy, whose stone wall, winding in and out of the trees, is worth the trip alone.

Further into the Catskills is the small town of Saugerties, the site of the second 1960s Woodstock rock festival and home to those quintessential American main streets. Yes, there are antiques shops but they are interspersed with a bay-windowed candy shop, a hardware store with its brightly colored wheelbarrows upended on the sidewalk and an old-fashioned cinema. The small selection of restaurants includes a great place called Café Tamayo, offering New American bistro fare in an interior decorated with 1800s paddle fans.

The Villa at Saugerties is a contemporary bed and breakfast in a 1929 Spanish-style villa with an ochre stucco exterior and red tile roof, set in a pastoral setting down a back road outside the town. Owners Aimee Szparaga and Richard Nocera are young Manhattanites who recently upped sticks to set up a "modern country escape." With its palette of grey and magenta, the living area has modern Danish pieces and features an exposed bluestone fireplace. Details such as bunches of fresh flowers, Jonathan Adler throw cushions and copies of *Visionaire* magazine ease discerning urbanites into their country refuge. In clement weather guests can eat breakfast underneath a spreading sycamore tree on the patio outside, near the pristine swimming pool.

Bucks County: Eccentricity and Antiques

- EverMay on the Delaware
- Fonthill
- Mercer Museum
- Golden Nugget Antique Flea Market
- Lambertville Antique Flea Market

The bucolic meadows, covered bridges and stone farmhouses of Bucks County in eastern Pennsylvania have long held artists and writers in their thrall. In the 1930s and 1940s, New York's literati made the towns dotted along the Delaware River the scene of their voluntary exile. Dorothy Parker, the acerbic wit of the Algonquin Round Table (see p. 74), gravitated to a 14-room manse in Piperville, and lyricist Oscar Hammerstein resettled on a farm in Doylestown. Today, while the town of New Hope has become rather touristy, there is still plenty for those drawn to whimsical history and antiques, or just beautiful countryside.

Install yourself at the EverMay on the Delaware, a three-story, 18-room inn dating from 1790 and set right beside the river. Each room, amply furnished with antiques, is named for a famous person in Bucks County history. The stately Colonel William Erwin room, for example, sports a baronial headboard and matching marble-topped bureau. The six-course, award-winning dinner is the work of chef Jeffrey Lauble.

Archaeologist, architect, fiddler, tilemaker and erudite collector, Henry Chapman Mercer left his mark firmly upon Doylestown, where he spent all of his life. Mercer's dream house – a demented sandcastle of a mansion named Fonthill – which he built by hand between 1908 and 1912, is made from hand-poured reinforced concrete. As a leading figure of the Arts and Crafts movement, he established a tilemaking factory and Fonthill is lined with his handmade colorful, often narrative-depicting tiles. The Mercer Museum holds his collection of more than 50,000 tools of early American crafts and trades and everyday household objects used in America from 1700 to 1850. To add to your own collection of Americana, cross the river to Lambertville, an unpretentious town with a colonial-village feel and the site of the famous Lambertville Antique Market and Golden Nugget Antique Flea Market, both on River Road.

Hudson River Valley: Ancient Landscape, Contemporary Art

- Dia:Beacon
- Pig Hill Inn
- East Side Kitchen

Beacon is a small 18th- and 19th-century town on the banks of the Hudson River, 60 miles (100 kilometers) and so many fashion cycles north of Manhattan. And yet this sleepy town is the new home of Dia's permanent collection of major works of art from the 1960s to the present and thus a new hot spot on the international map of contemporary art. The museum – collaboratively planned by Robert Irwin, and art legend and project architect, the New York-based Open Office – occupies a historic printing factory on the Hudson. The 1929 steel, concrete and glass factory building provides a superb environment for contemporary art. The gritty industrial town itself is of interest, too. A burgeoning art scene has brought artists and galleries to the warehouse buildings, and dozens of excellent antique shops flank the main street.

Beacon's riches do not, as yet, include any accommodations, so it is advisable to use as a base the quaint village of Cold Spring, some 10 miles (16 kilometers) to the south. Here, too, is a pleasing collection of antiques shops, bookstores and tearooms lining the main street under ornate cornices. But the real treat lies at the end of the street, where it meets the Hudson River. The views – of the stretch upstream and down where the river narrows and deepens and of the opposite bank, formed of primeval-looking masses of granite and dense green forest – are spectacular. Artists of the Hudson River School, such as Thomas Cole and Asher B. Durand, were similarly fascinated by this tract through the Appalachian Mountain range.

The Pig Hill Inn is the place to stay. Housed in an 1820 brick building on the main street, the inn has nine guest rooms, each appointed with antiques that are for sale, and most have wood stoves. Breakfast can be taken in your four-poster bed, the dining room or in the quiet garden out back. If you need a snack during the day, simply cross the street to the East Side Kitchen for a milkshake or burger in the playfully retro diner given a makeover by a couple of East Village musicians.

OCEANSIDE CHIC
East Hampton: Scene by the Sea
- Glen Horowitz Bookseller
- Jackson Pollock House and Studio
- The Dan Flavin Art Institute
- Sunset Beach Hotel
- The 1770 House

Long Island's East End beaches are gorgeous broad swaths of pale sand, backed with low picket fences and dune grasses. Between the months of May and September, however, they are littered with high-strung New Yorkers "getting away from it all." Enormous ersatz mansions replete with back-garden polo fields for the likes of Sean "Puffy" Combs and Steven Spielberg have replaced the once-flat open potato fields that unfolded to the Atlantic. And yet, the clear light, the charm of such villages as Amagansett and the exhilarating sense of escape at Montauk, the South Fork's tip, ensure that the Hamptons remain a lovely retreat, particularly during September. East Hampton, with its boutiques and specialty shops, is easily accessible by bus or train and provides a good base. Just to the north, in a rural hamlet called The Springs, is the cottage and studio where Jackson Pollock created his most important works between 1946 and his death ten years later. The house has been left beautifully intact so that you can still browse through the artist's large collection of jazz records and library and see the paint splatters on the floor. Bridgehampton, the next town to the west of East Hampton, is home to The Dan Flavin Art Institute, a permanent installation of nine of Flavin's works in fluorescent light in a renovated firehouse building.

Most New Yorkers rent houses in the summer, and for short stays there are only a handful of interesting lodgings. One such place is Andre Balazs's 20-luxury-room Sunset Beach Hotel on Shelter Island, situated between the North and South Forks of Long Island. Another option is The 1770 House on East Hampton's Main Street, within easy reach of the boutiques and the secluded Egypt beach. Designer Laura Maerov, who recently restored the inn, has combined traditional wallpapers, wood paneling and eclectic antiques to give each room individual charm. The destination restaurant serves seasonal American cuisine by local star chef, Kevin Penner.

contact

All telephone numbers are given for dialling locally, but a '1' must be dialled before the ten-digit number when calling from outside the area code (i.e., 212 or 718). From abroad, the country code is +1, followed by the ten-digit number, without another '1'. The same applies for telephone numbers in the retreat section. The number in brackets by the name is the page number on which the entry appears.

71 Clinton Fresh Food [60]
71 Clinton Street
New York, NY 10002
T   212 614 6960

Abyssinian Baptist Church [90]
132 Odell Clark Place
New York, NY 10030
T   212 862 7474
F   212 862 3255
E   info@abyssinian.org
W   www.abyssinian.org

aka Café [60]
49 Clinton Street
New York, NY 10002
T   212 979 6096

Albanese Meats & Poultry [21]
238 Elizabeth Street
New York, NY 10012
T   212 966 1788

Al di La [142]
248 5th Avenue
Brooklyn, NY 11215
T   718 783 4565
E   aldila@inch.com
W   www.aldilatrattoria.com

Algonquin Hotel [74]
59 West 44th Street
New York, NY 10036
T   212 840 6800
W   www.thealgonquin.net

Alpana Bawa [57]
70 East 1st Street
New York, NY 10003
T   212 254 1249
F   212 477 0131
E   alpanabawa@verizon.net
W   www.alpanabawa.com

American Folk Art Museum [75]
45 West 53rd Street
New York, NY 10019
T   212 265 1040
F   212 265 2350
E   info@folkartmuseum.org
W   www.folkartmuseum.org

Angel Orensanz Foundation Center for the Arts [60]
172 Norfolk Street
New York, NY 10002
T   212 529 7194
F   212 529 1864
E   info@orensanz.org
W   www.orensanz.org

Angel's Share [156]
8 Stuyvesant Street
New York, NY 10003
T   212 777 5415

Annex Antiques Fair and Flea Market [38]
Sixth Avenue between 24th and 26th Streets
New York, NY 10003
T   212 243 5343

Another Room [17]
249 West Broadway
New York, NY 10013
T   212 226 1418
W   www.anotheroomnyc.com

The Apartment [27]
101 Crosby Street
New York, NY 10012
T   212 219 3661
F   212 219 3683
E   speakout@theapt.com
W   www.theapt.com

The Apple Store [28]
103 Prince Street
New York, NY 10012
T   212 226 3126
W   www.apple.com/retail/soho

Artists Space [22]
38 Greene Street, 3rd Floor
New York, NY 10013
T   212 226 3970
F   212 966 1434
E   artspace@artistsspace.org
W   www.artistsspace.org

Asia Society [83]
725 Park Avenue
New York, NY 10021
T   212 288 6400
F   212 517 8315
E   info@asiasoc.org
W   www.asiasociety.org

Auto [167]
805 Washington Street
New York, NY 10014
T   212 229 2292
F   212 229 0002
E   shop@thisisauto.com
W   www.thisisauto.com

Balthazar [22]
80 Spring Street
New York, NY 10012
T   212 965 1785
F   212 966 2502
E   frontdesk@balthazarny.com
W   www.balthazarny.com

Bar 89 [22]
89 Mercer Street
New York, NY 10012
T   212 274 0989

The Bar Room at the Modern [69]
9 West 53rd Street
New York, NY 10019
T   212 333 1220
W   www.themodernnyc.com

Barney Greengrass Sturgeon King [136]
541 Amsterdam Avenue
New York, NY 10024
T   212 724 4707
F   212.595 6565
E   info@barneygreengrass.com
W   www.barneygreengrass.com

Barneys [162]
660 Madison Avenue
New York, NY 10021
T   212 826 8900
W   www.barneys.com

Barneys Co-op [162]
236 West 18th Street
New York, NY 10011
116 Wooster Street
New York, NY 10012
T   212 593 7800
W   www.barneys.com

A Bathing Ape [22]
91 Greene Street
New York, NY 10012
T   212 925 0222

Bayard Building [31]
65 Bleecker Street
New York, NY 10012

B–Bar & Grill [158]
40 East 4th Street
New York, NY 10003
T   212 475 2220
F   212 475 9269
W   www.bbarandgrill.com

Bed and Breakfast on the Park [116]
113 Prospect Park West
Brooklyn, NY 11215
T   718 499 6115
W   www.bbnyc.com

Bemelmans Bar [84]
Ground Floor of Carlyle Hotel
35 East 76th Street
New York, NY 10021
T   212 744 1600
W   www.thecarlyle.com

Bid [83]
1334 York Avenue
New York, NY 10021
T   212 988 7730

The Biltmore Room [37]
290 Eighth Avenue
New York, NY 10001
T   212 807 0111
W   www.thebiltmoreroom.com

Bohemian Hall & Beer Garden [157]
29–19 24th Avenue
Astoria, NY 11102
T   718 274 4925
F   718 728 9278
E   manager@bohemianhall.com
W   www.bohemianhall.com

Bond 07 [168]
7 Bond Street
New York, NY 10012
T   212 677 8487
F   212 677 7872
W   www.selimaoptique.com

Bottino [40]
246 Tenth Avenue
New York, NY 10001
T   212 206 6766
E   info@bottinonyc.com
W   www.bottinonyc.com

Bouley [16]
120 West Broadway
New York, NY 10013
T   212 964 2525
F   212 219 3443
E   info@bouleynyc.com
W   www.bouley.net

Brasserie [73]
100 East 53rd Street
New York, NY 10022
T   212 751 4840
W   www.restaurantassociates.com/brasserie

Bridge Café [62]
279 Water Street
New York, NY 10038
T   212 227 3344
F   212 619 2368
E   bridgecafechef@aol.com

The Broken Kilometer [28]
393 West Broadway
New York, NY 10012
W   www.diacenter.org

Brooklyn Academy of Music [111]
30 Lafayette Avenue
Brooklyn, NY 11217
T   718 636 4100
E   info@bam.org
W   www.bam.org

Brooklyn Botanic Garden [108]
1000 Washington Avenue
Brooklyn, NY 11225
T   718 623 7200
W   www.bbg.org

Brooklyn Inn [108]
148 Hoyt Street
Brooklyn, NY 11217
T   718 625 9741

Brooklyn Museum of Art [108]
200 Eastern Parkway
Brooklyn, NY 11238
T   718 638 5000
F   718 501 6136
E   information@brooklynmuseum.org
W   www.brooklynart.org

Brooklyn Social [157]
335 Smith Street
Brooklyn, NY 11231
T   718 858 7758

Brown + Orange [62]
61 Hester Street
New York, NY 10002
T   212 254 9825

Café des Artistes [88]
1 West 67th Street
New York, NY 10023
T   212 877 3500
F   212 877 6263
W   www.cafedesartistesnyc.com

Café Gitane [146]
242 Mott Street
New York, NY 10012
T   212 334 9552

Café Habana [21]
17 Prince Street
New York, NY 10012
T   212 625 2002
F   212 625 3663

Café Luxembourg [89]
200 West 70th Street
New York, NY 10023
T   212 873 7411
F   212 721 6854

Café Sabarsky [87]
Neue Galerie
1048 Fifth Avenue
New York, NY, 10028
T   212 288 0665
F   212 645 7127
W   www.wallserestaurant.com

Caffé Roma [154]
385 Broome Street
New York, NY 10013
T   212 226 8413

Campbell Apartment [68]
Grand Central Terminal
15 Vanderbilt Avenue
New York, NY 10017
T   212 953 0409

Castor and Pollux [174]
67 1/2 Sixth Avenue
Brooklyn, NY 10013
T/F 718 398 4141

Chanterelle [16]
2 Harrison Street
New York, NY 10013
T   212 966 6960
F   212 966 6143
E   information@chanterellenyc.com
W   www.chanterellenyc.com

Chelsea Market [38]
75 Ninth Avenue
New York, NY 10011
W   www.chelseamarket.com

Chibi's Sake Bar [155]
238 Mott Street
New York, NY 10012
T   212 274 0054
W   www.chibisbar.com

ChiKaLicious [56]
203 East 10th Street
New York, NY 10003
T   212 995 9511
E   info@chikalicious.com
W   www.chikalicious.com

Chrysler Building [70]
405 Lexington Avenue
New York, NY 10174
T   212 682 3070

Church Lounge [18]
TriBeCa Grand Hotel
2 Sixth Avenue
New York, NY 10013
T   212 519 6677
E   churchlounge@tribecagrand.com
W   www.tribecagrand.com

Cielo [44]
18 Little West 12th Street
New York, NY 10014
T   212 645 5700
F   212 654 0051
W   www.cieloclub.com

City Bakery [55]
3 West 18th Street
New York, NY 10011
T   212 366 1414
W   www.thecitybakery.com

City Club Hotel [120]
55 West 44th Street
New York, NY 10036
T   212 921 5500
F   212 944 5544
W   www.cityclubhotel.com

C.O. Bigelow Apothecaries [48]
414 Sixth Avenue
New York, NY 10011
T   212 533 2700
W   www.bigelowchemists.com

Comme des Garçons [43]
520 West 22nd Street
New York, NY 10011
T   212 604 9200

Commissary [83]
1030 Third Avenue
New York, NY 10021
T   212 339 9955
F   212 339 0015

Community Garden [57]
East 6th Street and Avenue B
New York, NY 10009
E   info@6bgarden.org
W   www.6bgarden.org

Conservatory Gardens [87]
Central Park
Fifth Avenue at East 105th Street
New York, NY 10029
W   www.centralpark.org

**Cooper-Hewitt National
Design Museum** [84]
2 East 91st Street
New York, NY 10128
T   212 849 8400
W   www.ndm.si.edu

Corner Bistro [140]
331 West 4th Street
New York, NY 10014
T/F 212 242 9502

Craft [146]
43 East 19th Street
New York, NY 10003
T   212 780 0880

**Deadly Dragon Sound
System** [62]
102-B Forsyth Street
New York, NY 10002
T   646 613 0139
E   deadlydragonsoun@gmail.com
W   www.deadlydragonsound.com

Decibel [57]
240 East 9th Street
New York 10003
T   212 979 2733

Deitch Projects [25]
76 Grand Street
New York, NY 10013
T   212 343 7300
F   212 343 2954
18 Wooster Street
New York, NY 10013
T   212 941 9475
E   email@deitch.com
W   www.deitch.com

DIA Center for the Arts [41]
545 & 548 West 22nd Street
New York, NY 10011
T   212 989 5566
F   212 989 4055
E   info@diaart.org
W   www.diacenter.org

Diane von Furstenberg [48]
385 West 12th Street
New York, NY 10014
T   646 486 4800
W   www.dvf.com

Diner [138]
85 Broadway
Brooklyn, NY 11211
T   718 486 3077

Donald Judd House [24]
101 Spring Street
New York, NY 10012

Double Happiness [18]
173 Mott Street

New York, NY 10013
T   212 941 1282

Doughnut Plant [60]
379 Grand Street
New York, NY 10002
T/F 212 505 3700
E   staff@doughnutplant.com
W   www.doughnutplant.com

DUMBO General Store [102]
111 Front Street
Brooklyn, NY 11201
T   718 855 5288
W   www.dumbogeneralstore.com

Dumpling House [60]
118a Eldridge Street
New York, NY 10002
T   212 625 8008

Economy Candy [58]
108 Rivington Street
New York, NY 10002
T   212 254 1832
F   212 254 2606
E   thestore@economycandy.com
W   www.economycandy.com

El Quijote [43]
226 West 23rd Street
New York, NY 10011
T   212 929 1855

Employees Only [156]
510 Hudson Street
New York, NY 10014
T   212 242 3021
E   info@employeesonlynyc.com
W   www.employeesonlynyc.com

Fanelli's [27]
94 Prince Street
New York, NY 10012
T   212 226 9412

Flight 001 [48]
96 Greenwich Avenue
New York, NY 10011
T   212 691 1001
F   212 691 8660
E   info@flight001.com
W   www.flight001.com

Florent [47]
69 Gansevoort Street
New York, NY 10014
T   212 989 5779
F   212 645 2498
W   www.restaurantflorent.com

Four Seasons Bar [159]
Seagram Building
99 East 52nd Street
New York, NY 10022
T   212 754 9494
F   212 754 1077
W   www.fourseasons
    restaurant.com

Frank's Lounge [111]
660 Fulton Street
Brooklyn, NY 11238

T   718 625 9339
W   www.frankscocktail
    lounge.com

Fraunces Tavern [62]
54 Pearl Street
New York, NY 10004
T   212 968 1776
F   212 797 1776
W   www.frauncestavern.com

Freeman's [137]
2 Freeman Alley
New York, NY 10012
T   212 420 0012

The Frick Collection [83]
1 East 70th Street
New York, NY 10021
T   212 288 0700
F   212 628 4417
E   info@frick.org
W   www.frick.org

The Future Perfect [166]
115 North 6th Street
Brooklyn, NY 11211
T   718 599 6278
E   info@thefutureperfect.com
W   www.thefutureperfect.com

Gagosian Gallery [37]
555 West 24th Street
New York, NY 10011
T   212 741 1111
F   212 741 9611
E   info@gagosian.com
W   www.gagosian.com

Galapagos [99]
70 North 6th Street
Brooklyn, NY 11211
T   718 782 5188
E   info@galapagosartspace.com
W   www.galapagosartspace.com

**Gavin Brown's
Enterprise** [17]
620 Greenwich Street
New York, NY 10014
T   212 627 5258
F   212 627 5261
E   gallery@gavinbrown.biz
W   www.gavinbrown.biz

**Good World Barber
Shop** [150]
3 Orchard Street
New York, NY 10003
T   212 925 9975
W   www.goodworldbar.com

Gramercy Tavern [55]
42 East 20th Street
New York, NY 10003
T   212 477 0777
F   212 477 1160
E   info@gramercytavern.com
W   www.gramercytavern.com

**The Grand Central Oyster
Bar & Restaurant** [141]
Grand Central Station

Lower Concourse
42nd Street
New York, NY 10017
T   212 490 6650
F   212 949 5210
E   info@oysterbarny.com
W   www.oysterbarny.com

Greenmarket [56]
Union Square
East 17th Street and Broadway
New York, NY 10003
T   212 788 7476
E   info@greenmarket.cc
W   www.cenyc.org

The Grocery [108]
288 Smith Street
Brooklyn, NY 11231
T   718 596 3335

Guastavino's [84]
409 East 59th Street
New York, NY 10022
T   212 980 2455
F   212 980 2904
E   reservations1@
    guastavinos.com
W   www.guastavinos.com

**Helmut Lang
Parfumerie** [28]
81 Greene Street
New York, NY 10012
T   212 334 3921
F   212 334 3922
W   www.helmutlang.com

**Henry Urbach
Architecture** [38]
526 West 26th Street, 10th Floor
New York, NY 10001
T   212 627 0974
F   212 645 7222
E   hua@huagallery.com
W   www.huagallery.com

Hollywould [21]
198 Elizabeth Street
New York, NY 10012
T   212 343 8344
F   212 343 8345
E   shop@ilovehollywould.com
W   www.ilovehollywould.com

Honmura An [28]
170 Mercer Street
New York, NY 10012
T   212 334 5253

Hotel Chelsea [130]
222 West 23rd Street
New York, NY 10011
T   212 243 3700
F   212 675 5531
W   www.hotelchelsea.com

Hotel Gansevoort [132]
18 Ninth Avenue
New York, NY 10014
T   212 206 6700
F   212 255 5858

E contact@hotelgansevoort.com
W www.hotelgansevoort.com

Hotel on Rivington [124]
107 Rivington Street
New York, NY 10002
T 212 475 2600
F 212 475 5959
E info@hotelonrivington.com
W www.hotelonrivington.com

I Heart [175]
262 Mott Street
New York, NY 10012
T 212 219 9265

INA [21]
Women's:
21 Prince Street
New York, NY 10012
T 212 334 9048
Men's:
262 Mott Street
New York, NY 10012
T 212 334 2210

The Inn at Irving Place [122]
56 Irving Place
New York, NY 10003
T 212 533 4600
F 212 533 4611
E innatirving@aol.com
W www.innatirving.com

ISA [163]
88 North 6th Street
Brooklyn, NY 11211
T 718 387 3363
F 718 387 3464

Isamu Noguchi Garden Museum [102]
9-01 33rd Road
Long Island City, NY 11106
W www.noguchi.org

Jack Spade [170]
56 Greene Street
New York, NY 10012
T 212 625 1820
F 212 925 8477
W www.jackspade.com

Jack's Luxury Oyster Bar [144]
246 East 5th Street
New York, NY 10003
T 212 673 0338

Jaques Torres [102]
66 Water Street
Brooklyn, NY 11201
T 718 875 9772
F 718 875 2167
E info@mrchocolate.com
W www.jacquestorres.com

Jeffrey [47]
449 West 14th Street
New York, NY 10014
T 212 206 1272

Joe's Pub [31]
425 Lafayette Street
New York, NY 10003
T 212 539 8770
E info@joespub.com
W www.joespub.com

Juniors [111]
386 Flatbush Avenue
Brooklyn, NY 11238
T 718 852 5257

Kate Spade Travel [165]
59 Thompson Street
New York, NY 10012
T 212 965 8654
F 212 965 8653
W www.katespade.com

Katz's Delicatessen [145]
205 East Houston Street
New York, NY 10002
T 212 254 2246
W www.katzdeli.com

Kidrobot [25]
126 Prince Street
New York, NY 10012
T 212 966 6688
W nystore@kidrobot.com
W www.kidrobot.com

Kiehl's [169]
109 Third Avenue
New York, NY 10003
T 212 677 3171
W www.kiehls.com

King Cole Bar and Lounge [155]
St. Regis Hotel
2 East 55th Street
New York NY 10022
T 212 753 4500
F 212 787 3447
W www.starwood.com/stregis

Kinokuniya [76]
10 West 49th Street
New York, NY 10020
T 212 765 7766
F 212 541 9335
E kinokuniya@kinokuniya.com
W www.kinokuniya.com

Kirna Zabete [164]
96 Greene Street
New York, NY 10012
T 212 941 9656
E info@kirnazabete.com
W www.kirnazabete.com

Knitting Factory [18]
74 Leonard Street
New York, NY 10013
T 212 219 3132
W www.knittingfactory.com

La Lunchonette [44]
130 Tenth Avenue
New York, NY 10011
T 212 675 0342

Layla [108]
86 Hoyt Street
Brooklyn, NY 11201
T 718 222 1933

Lenox Lounge [90]
288 Lenox Avenue (Malcolm X Boulevard)
New York, NY 10027
T 212 427 0253
E info@lenoxlounge.com
W www.lenoxlounge.com

Lever House Restaurant [143]
360 Park Avenue
New York, NY 10022
T 212 888 2700
F 212 888 2740
E info@leverhouse.com
W www.leverhouse.com

Li-Lac Chocolates, Inc. [48]
120 Christopher Street
New York, NY 10014
T 212 242 7374
F 212 366 5874

Lincoln Center for the Performing Arts [89]
65th Street at Columbus Avenue
New York, NY 10023
T 212 875 5456
E webmaster@lincolncenter.org
W www.lincolncenter.org

Linda Dresner [73]
484 Park Avenue
New York, NY 10022
T 212 308 3177
F 212.755.6737
E info@lindadresner.com
W www.lindadresner.com

Liz Christy Garden [31]
Northeast corner of Houston and Bowery Streets
New York, NY 10013
W www.lizchristygarden.org

Lot 61 [43]
550 West 21st Street
New York, NY 10011
T 212 243 6555
W www.lot61.com

Louis Vuitton [73]
1 East 57th Street
New York, NY 10022
T 212 758 8877
F 212 758 8882
E contact@louisvuitton.com
W www.vuitton.com

Lovely Day [21]
196 Elizabeth Street
New York, NY 10012
T 212 925 3310

The Lowell [128]
28 East 63rd Street
New York, NY 10021

T 212 838 1400
F 212 605 6808

Lower East Side Tenement Museum [60]
90 Orchard Street
New York, NY 10002
T 212 431 0233
F 212 431 0402
E lestm@tenement.org
W www.tenement.org

Lucy Barnes [48]
320 West 14th Street
New York, NY 10014
T 212 255 9502
F 212 255 5160

Luhring Augustine [38]
531 West 24th Street
New York, NY 10011
T 212 206 9100
F 212 206 9055
E info@luhringaugustine.com
W www.luhringaugustine.com

LVMH Tower [73]
19–21 East 57th Street
New York, NY 10022
T 212 931 2000
F 212 931 2903

Lyell [21]
173 Elizabeth Street
New York, NY 10012
T 212 966 8484

Magnolia Bakery [48]
401 Bleecker Street
New York, NY 10014
T 212 462 2572

Malin + Goetz [43]
177 Seventh Avenue
New York, NY 10011
T 212 727 3777
W www.malinandgoetz.com

Marc Jacobs [172]
Ready-to-wear & men's:
163 Mercer Street
New York, NY 10012
Accessories & shoes:
385 Bleecker Street
New York, NY 10014
Marc by Marc Jacobs:
403–5 Bleecker Street
New York, NY 10014
T 212 924 0026
W www.marcjacobs.com

The Maritime Hotel [118]
363 West 16th Street
New York, NY 10011
T 212 242 4300
F 212 242 1188
W www.themaritimehotel.com

Matthew Marks Gallery [38]
523 West 24th Street
New York, NY 10011
T 212 243 0200

E info@matthewmarks.com
W www.matthewmarks.com

Maxilla and Mandible [87]
451 Columbus Avenue
New York, NY 10024
T 212 724 6173
F 212 721 1073
E maxilla@maxillaand
mandible.com
W www.maxillaand
mandible.com

Max Protetch Gallery [41]
511 West 22nd Street
New York, NY 10011
T 212 633 6999
F 212 691 4342
E info@maxprotech.com
W www.maxprotech.com

Mayle [173]
252 Elizabeth Street
New York, NY 10012
T 212 625 0406

McSorley's Old Ale House [151]
15 East 7th Street
New York, NY 10003
T 212 473 9148

Me & Ro [169]
241 Elizabeth Street
New York, NY 10012
T 917 237 9215
F 917 237 9219
E meandrony@
meandrojewelry.com
W www.meandrojewelry.com

Meet [46]
71–73 Gansevoort Street
New York, NY 10014
T 212 242 0990
F 212 242 1952
E info@the-meet.com
W www.the-meet.com

Megu [140]
62 Thomas Street
New York, NY 10013
T 212 964 7777
F 212 964 7776
E info@megunyc.com.com
W www.foodscope.com

Merc Bar [27]
151 Mercer Street
New York, NY 10012
T 212 966 2727
F 212 996 3329
W info@mercbar.com
W www.mercbar.com

Mercedes-Benz Showroom [73]
430 Park Avenue
New York, NY 10022
T 212 629 1666

Merchant's House Museum [31]
29 East 4th Street
New York, NY 10003
T 212 777 1089
F 212 777 1104
E nyc1832@
merchantshouse.com
W www.merchantshouse.com

The Metropolitan Museum of Art [84]
1000 Fifth Avenue
New York, NY 10028
T 212 535 7710
W www.metmuseum.org

Mies + Design Shop [76]
319 West 47th Street
New York, NY 10036
T 212 247 3132

MoMA Design and Book Store [175]
44 West 53rd Street
New York, NY 10019
T 212 708 9400

Momenta Art [98]
72 Berry Street
Brooklyn, NY 11211
T 718 218 8058
W www.momentaart.org

The Morgan Library [68]
29 East 36th Street
New York, NY 10016
T 212 685 0610
W www.morganlibrary.org

Moss [167]
146 Greene Street
New York, NY 10012
T 212 204 7100
F 212 204 7101
E customerservice@
mossonline.com
W www.mossonline.com

Moto [101]
394 Broadway
Brooklyn, NY 11211
T 718 599 6895
W www.circa1938.com

The Museum of Modern Art [69]
11 West 53rd Street
New York, NY 10019
T 212 708 9400
E info@moma.org
W www.moma.org

National Arts Club [55]
15 Gramercy Park South
New York, NY 10003
T 212 475 3424
W www.nationalartsclub.org

Neue Galerie [87]
1048 Fifth Avenue
New York, NY 10028
T 212 628 6200

F 212 628 8824
E museum@neuegalerie.org
W www.neuegalerie.org

The New York Earth Room [28]
141 Wooster Street
New York, NY 10012
W www.diacenter.org

New York Public Library [70]
Fifth Avenue and 42nd Street
New York, NY 10018
T 212 930 0830
W www.nypl.org

New York Stock Exchange [62]
8 Broad Street
New York, NY 10005
T 212 56 5168
W www.nyse.com

Nom de Guerre [31]
640 Broadway
New York, NY 10012
T 212 253 2891

Odeon [141]
145 West Broadway
New York, NY 10013
T 212 233 0507

Other Music [31]
15 East 4th Street
New York, NY 10003
T 212 477 8150
W www.othermusic.com

Ouest [89]
2315 Broadway
New York, NY 10024
T 212 580 8700
F 212 580 1360
W www.ouestny.com

Oznot's Dish [98]
79 Berry Street
Brooklyn, NY 11211
T 718 599 6596

Paley Park [69]
5 East 53rd Street
New York, NY 10022

The Park [152]
118 Tenth Avenue
New York, NY 10011
T 212 352 3313

Passerby [154]
436 West 15th Street
New York, NY 10011
T 212 206 7321

Pastis [46]
9 Ninth Avenue
New York, NY 10014
T 212 929 4844

Pearl River Mart [18]
477 Broadway
New York, NY 10013
T 212 431 4770
E info@pearlriver.com
W www.pearlriver.com

Peking Duck House [18]
28 Mott Street
New York, NY 10013
T 212 227 1810

Peter Luger's Steak House [139]
178 Broadway
Brooklyn, NY 11211
T 718 387 7400
F 718 387 3523
E info@peterluger.com
W www.peterluger.com

Pete's Candy Store [97]
709 Lorimer Street
Brooklyn, NY 11211
T 718 302 3770
W www.petescandystore.com

Pete's Tavern [55]
129 East 18th Street
New York, NY 10003
T 212 473 7676
W www.petestavern.com

Pierogi 2000 [99]
177 North 9th Street
Brooklyn, NY 11211
T 718 599 2144
W www.pierogi2000.com

Pop Burger [43]
58-60 Ninth Avenue
New York, NY 10011
T 212 414 8686

Prada [170]
575 Broadway
New York, NY 10012
T 212 334 8888

Printed Matter, Inc. [40]
535 West 22nd Street
New York, NY 10011
T 212 925 0325
F 212 925 0464
W www.printedmatter.org

P.S.1 Contemporary Art Center [102]
22–25 Jackson Avenue
Long Island City, NY 11101
T 718 784 2084
F 718 482 9454
E mail@ps1.org
W www.ps1.org

Public [147]
210 Elizabeth Street
New York, NY 10012
T 212 343 7011
F 212 343 0918
W www.public-nyc.com

Rainbow Grill [76]
30 Rockefeller Plaza
65th Floor
New York, NY 10012
T 212 632 5100
F 212 632 5105
E reservations@cipriani.com
W www.cipriani.com/cipriani/
   RainbowGrill/grill.htm

Ralph Lauren [83]
867 Madison Avenue
New York, NY 10022
T 212 606 2100
W www.polo.com

The Red Cat [44]
227 Tenth Avenue
New York, NY 10011
T 212 242 1122
F 212 242 1390
W www.theredcat.com

Red Flower [28]
13 Prince Street
New York, NY 10012
T 212 966 1994
F 212 966 2180
W www.redflower.com

Relish [101]
225 Wythe Avenue
Brooklyn, NY 11211
T 718 963 4546
W www.relish.com

**The Roosevelt Island
Tramway** [84]
59th Street and Second Avenue
W www.rioc.com

Russ & Daughters [58]
179 East Houston Street
New York, NY 10002
T 212 475 4880
F 212 475 0345
E info@russanddaughters.com
W www.russanddaughters.com

Russian Samovar [75]
256 West 52nd Street
New York, NY 10019
T 212 757 0168
F 212 765 2133
E info@russiansamovar.com
W www.russiansamovar.com

St. Mark's Bookshop [56]
31 Third Avenue
New York, NY 10003
T 212 260 7853
F 212 598 4950
E stmarksbooks@
   mindspring.com
W www.stmarksbookshop.com

Scalo [43]
436 West 15th Street
New York, NY 10011
T 212 627 9991
F 212 627 0700
W www.scalo.com

Schiller's Liquor Bar [58]
131 Rivington Street
New York, NY 10002
T 212 260 4555
E info@schillersny.com

Sculpture Center [102]
44-19 Purves Street
Long Island City, NY 11101
T 718 361 1750
F 718 786 9336
E info@sculpture-center.org
W www.sculpture-center.org

Seize Sur Vingt [171]
243 Elizabeth Street
New York, NY 10012
T 212 343 0476
F 212 348 9589
E nyc@16sur20.com
W www.16sur20.com

**Seventh Regiment
Armory** [84]
640 Park Avenue
New York, NY 10021

**Sherwood Cafe at Robin
des Bois** [153]
195 Smith Street
Brooklyn, NY 11201
T 718 596 1609
W www.sherwoodcafe.com

Sigerson Morrison [164]
28 Prince Street
New York, NY 10012
T 212 219 3893
W www.sigersonmorrison.com

Single Room Occupancy
[150]
360 West 53rd Street
New York, NY 10019
T 212 765 6299

Sixty Thompson [126]
60 Thompson Street
New York, NY 10012
T 212 204 6465
F 212 431 0200
E info@thompsonhotels.com
W www.60thompson.com

Skyscraper Museum [62]
39 Battery Place
New York, NY 10280
T 212 968 1961
W www.skyscraper.org

**Socrates Sculpture
Park** [97]
Broadway and Vernon Boulevard
Long Island City, NY 11106
T 718 956 1819
F 718 626 1533
E info@socratessculpturepark.
   org
W www.socratessculpturepark.
   org

**Solomon R. Guggenheim
Museum** [87]
1071 Fifth Avenue
New York, NY 10128
T 212 423 3500
W www.guggenheim.org

Spoonbill & Sugartown [101]
218 Bedford Avenue
Brooklyn, NY 11211
T 718 387 7322
E info@spoonbillbooks.com
W www.spoonbillbooks.com

Spring [102]
126a Front Street
Brooklyn, NY 11201
T 718 222 1054
W www.spring3d.net

**Starrett Lehigh
Building** [38]
601 West 26th Street
New York, NY 10001

Steinway & Sons [76]
109 West 57th Street
New York, NY 10019
T 212 246 1100
W www.steinway.com

Steven Alan [165]
103 Franklin Street
New York, NY 10013
T 212 343 0692
F 212 343 8847
E orders@stevenalan.com
W www.stevenalan.com

Steven Salen Tailors [70]
18 East 53rd Street
New York, NY 10022
T 212 755 5665

**Storefront for Art
and Architecture** [18]
97 Kenmare Street
New York, NY 10012
T 212 431 5795
F 212 431 5755
E info@storefrontnews.org
W www.storefrontnews.org

**The Studio Museum in
Harlem** [90]
144 West 125th Street (Dr. Martin
Luther King, Jr. Boulevard)
New York, NY 10027
T 212 864 4500
F 212 864 4800
W www.studiomuseum.org

Supreme [24]
274 Lafayette Street
New York, NY 10012
T 212 966 7799
F 212 966 7907

**Sylvia's Soul Food
Restaurant** [90]
328 Lenox Avenue
(Malcolm X Boulevard)
New York, NY 10027

T 212 996 0660
F 212 427 6389
W www.sylviassoulfood.com

Tabla [55]
11 Madison Avenue
New York, NY 10010
T 212 889 0667
F 212 889 0914
W www.tablany.com

Takashimaya [74]
693 Fifth Avenue
New York, NY 10022
T 212 350 0100
F 212 350 0542
W www.ny-takashimaya.com

Teany [150]
90 Rivington Street
New York, NY 10002
T 212 475 9190
W www.teany.com

Ted Muehling [22]
27 Howard Street
New York, NY 10013
T 212 431 3825
W www.tedmuehling.com

Temple Bar [159]
332 Lafayette Street
New York, NY 10012
T 212 925 4242
W www.templebarnyc.com

TG170 [60]
170 Ludlow Street
New York, NY 10002
T 212 995 8660
F 212 533 4945
E info@tg170.com
W www.tg170.com

Thomas Beisl [111]
25 Lafayette Avenue
Brooklyn, NY 11217
T 718 222 5800

Tiffany & Co. [73]
727 Fifth Avenue
New York, NY 10022
T 212 755 8000
W www.tiffany.com

TRASH [101]
256 Grand Street
Brooklyn, NY 11211
T 718 599 1000
W www.thetrashbar.com

TriBeCa Issey Miyake [17]
119 Hudson Street
New York, NY 10013
T 212 226 0100
F 212 428 6758
W www.isseymiyake.com

Unis [21]
226 Elizabeth Street
New York, NY 10012
T 212 431 5533

United Nations Headquarters [70]
First Avenue at 46th Street
New York, NY 10017
T   212 963 8687
E   unitg@un.org
W   www.un.org/tours

Urban Center Books [73]
457 Madison Avenue
New York, NY 10022
T   212 935 3595
F   212 223 2887
E   info@urbancenterbooks.com
W   www.urbancenterbooks.com

Ursus Rare Books [84]
Mezzanine of Carlyle Hotel
981 Madison Avenue
New York, NY 10021
T   212 772 8787
F   212 737 9306
E   ursus@ursusbooks.com
W   www.ursusbooks.com

Vesuvio Bakery Shop [28]
160 Prince Street
New York, NY 10012
T   212 925 8248

Visionaire [22]
11 Mercer Street
New York, NY 10013
T   212 274 8959
F   212 343 2595
E   info@visionaireworld.com
W   www.visionaireworld.com

Vitra Showroom [48]
29 Ninth Avenue
New York, NY 10014
T   212 929 3626
F   212 929 6424
W   www.vitra.com

Watts on Smith [108]
248 Smith Street
Brooklyn, NY 11231
T   718 596 2359
E   info@wattsonsmith.com
W   www.wattsonsmith.com

WD–50 [60]
50 Clinton Street
New York, NY 10002
T   212 477 2900
W   www.wd-50.com

Wild Lily Tearoom [43]
511–A West 22nd Street
New York, NY 10011
T   212 691 2258
F   212 691 7985
W   www.wildlilytearoom.com

Zabar's [88]
2245 Broadway
New York, NY 10024
T   212 787 2000
F   212 580 4477
E   info@zabars.com
W   www.zabars.com

Zakka [28]
147 Grand Street
New York, NY 10013
T   212 431 3961
E   info@zakkacorp.com
W   www.zakkacorp.com

Ziegfeld Theater [76]
141 West 54th Street
New York, NY 10019
T   212 765 7601
W   www.clearviewcinemas.com

CATSKILLS [178]
*Saugerties does not have a train
station, but from Penn Station you
can take the Amtrak rail line to
Rhinecliff (15 miles (24 kilometers)
to the east of Saugerties) or from
Grand Central Station the
MetroNorth commuter service to
Poughkeepsie, then get a taxi to
Saugerties. By car, the drive takes
an hour and forty-five minutes up
the west side of the Hudson River
along the Palisades Parkway and
then the New York State Thruway
North (I-87). The Villa at Saugerties
is a couple of miles outside the
town. For detailed directions use
their website.*

Storm King Art Center
Old Pleasant Hill Road
Mountainville, NY 10953
T   845 534 3115
F   845 534 4457
W   www.stormking.org
*Open April–December,
Wednesday–Sunday*

Café Tamayo
89 Partition Street
Saugerties, NY 12477
T   845 246 9371
E   tamayo@ulster.net
W   www.cafetamayo.com

The Villa at Saugerties
159 Fawn Road
Saugerties, NY 12477
T   845 246 0682
E   upstatevilla@aol.com
W   www.thevillaatsaugerties.com
Rooms from $140

BUCKS COUNTY [180]
*If you are not driving, take the bus
from Port Authority bus station,
Manhattan, to Frenchtown,
Pennsylvania. Take a taxi one mile
(1.6 kilometers) to the EverMay on
the Delaware in the village of
Erwinna. Bus schedules can be
found at www.transbridgebus.com/
sched_frenchny.htm*

EverMay on the Delaware
River Road
Erwinna, PA 18920
T   610 294 9100

E   info@evermay.com
W   www.evermay.com
Rooms from $160

Fonthill
East Court Street and Route 313
Doylestown, PA 18901
T   215 348 9461
E   fhmail@fonthillmuseum.org
W   www.mercermuseum.org/
fonthill

The Mercer Museum
84 South Pine Street.
Doylestown, PA 18901
T   215 345 0210
F   215 230 0823
E   info@mercermuseum.org
W   www.mercermuseum.org/
mercermuseum

Golden Nugget Antique Flea
Market
1850 River Road
Lambertville, NJ 08530
T   609 397 0811
E   info@gnmarket.com
W   www.gnmarket.com

Lambertville Antique Flea Market
1864 River Road
Lambertville, NJ 08530
T   609 397 0456

HUDSON RIVER VALLEY [182]
*Take the MetroNorth rail service
from Grand Central Station to
Beacon and then take it one stop
back towards New York to Cold
Spring. By car, take Palisades
Parkway North, cross Bear
Mountain Bridge and take Route 9D
north to Beacon. The journey is
approximately 90 minutes.*

Dia:Beacon
3 Beekman Street
Beacon, NY 12508
T   845 440 0100
F   845 440 0092
E   info@diabeacon.org
W   www.diabeacon.org

Pig Hill Inn
73 Main Street
Cold Spring, NY 10516
T   845 265 9247
E   pighillinn@aol.com
W   www.pighillinn.com
Rooms from $145

East Side Kitchen
124 Main Street
Cold Spring, NY 10516
T   845 265 7223
F   845 265 7224

EAST HAMPTON [184]
*By car, take the I-27 along the
south fork of Long Island to
.Bridgehampton and East Hampton.
For Shelter Island, take the ferry
from Sag Harbor. The train journey*

*from Penn Station to East Hampton
on the LIRR takes about two and a
half hours: further information is
available by calling 718 217 5477.
You can also take the Hampton
Jitney bus: information and details
on 631 283 4600 or 800 936 0440.*

Glen Horowitz Bookseller
87 Newtown Lane
East Hampton, NY 11937
T   631 324 5511

Pollock-Krasner House
830 Fireplace Road
East Hampton, NY 11937
T   631 324 4929
F   631 324 8768
W   www.pkhouse.org

The Dan Flavin Art Institute
Corwith Avenue off Main Street
Bridgehampton, NY 11932
T 631 537 1476
W   www.diacenter.org/ltproj/
flavbrid
Open May through September

Sunset Beach Hotel
35 Shore Road
Shelter Island, NY 11965
T   631 749 2001
F   631 749 1843
E   reservations@sunsetbeachli.
com
W   www.sunsetbeachli.com
Rooms from $245

1770 House
143 Main Street
East Hampton, NY 11937
T   631 324 1770
F   631 324 3504
E   innkeeper@1770house.com
W   www.1770house.com
Rooms from $250